BACK
TO THE
BIBLE

A CALL TO FOCUS OUR
MINDS ON THE WORD OF GOD

Published by
    Review and Herald® Publishing Association, Silver Spring, MD 20904

This book was:
    Copyedited by James Cavil, Cavil Copy Editing/Proofreading, LLC
    Interior and cover designed by Melinda Worden
    Cover illustration by Oleksandr—stock.adobe.com

Unless otherwise noted, Bible texts in this book are from the *Holy Bible, New International Version*. Copyright © 1973, 1978, 1984, 2011 by Biblica, Inc. Used by permission. All rights reserved worldwide.

Scripture quotations marked ESV are taken from *The Holy Bible*, English Standard Version, copyright © 2001 by Crossway Bibles, a division of Good News Publishers. Used by permission. All rights reserved.

Bible texts credited to KJV are from the King James Version of the Bible.

Scripture quotations marked NASB are from the *New American Standard Bible*, copyright © 1960, 1971, 1977, 1995, 2020 by The Lockman Foundation. All rights reserved.

Bible texts credited to NKJV are from the New King James Version. Copyright © 1979, 1980, 1982 by Thomas Nelson, Inc. Used by permission. All rights reserved.

Bible texts credited to RSV are from the Revised Standard Version of the Bible, copyright ©1946, 1952, 1971, by the Division of Christian Education of the National Council of the Churches of Christ in the U.S.A. Used by permission.

Printed in the U.S.A.

ISBN   978-0-8280-2945-2 (print)
        978-0-8127-0577-5 (ebook)

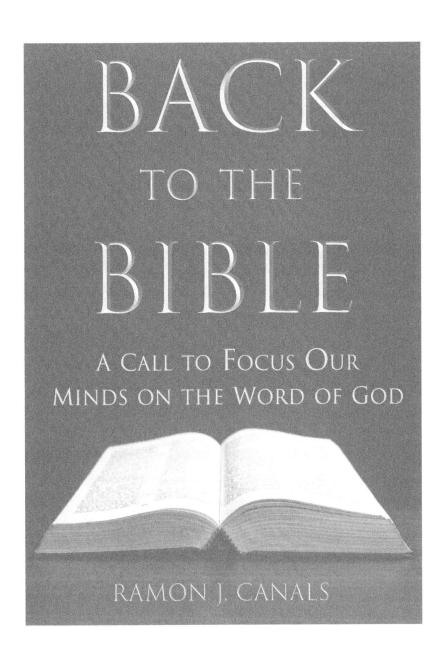

BACK
TO THE
BIBLE

A CALL TO FOCUS OUR MINDS ON THE WORD OF GOD

RAMON J. CANALS

Review&Herald®
PUBLISHING ASSOCIATION
SINCE 1861 | REVIEWANDHERALD.COM

FOREWORD

Have you ever wanted to increase your mental power, improve your memorization ability, enhance your focus during prayer, strengthen your connection with God, deepen your knowledge of the Bible, improve your ability to share God's truth with others, and increase your peace of mind? Ramón Canals, General Conference Ministerial secretary, offers you the opportunity to achieve all of that and much more in his fascinating book, *Back to the Bible*.

Too many people today are essentially illiterate when it comes to a careful rapport with and recollection of heavenly instruction in the Word of God. Through a careful approach to Bible study and a memorized repetition of texts in the Bible, you can experience a much higher focus on your relationship with Christ, His Word, and His purpose for your life as a soul winner and witness for Him.

In these last days of earth's history, we are to commit portions of Scripture to memory so that the Holy Spirit can help us recall them when we are faced with difficulties. In fact, the study of God's Holy Word will sharpen your mind greatly as you dig into the unlimited treasure house of the Bible. Pastor Canals shares this reassuring quote from Ellen White: "The Bible is the only rule of faith and doctrine. And there is nothing more calculated to energize the mind, and strengthen the intellect, than the study of the Word of God. No other book is so potent to elevate the thoughts, to give vigor to the faculties, as the broad, ennobling truths of the Bible. If God's Word were studied as it should be, men would have a breadth of mind, a nobility of character, and a stability of purpose, that is rarely seen in these times" (in *Review and Herald*, July 17, 1888).

In very practical and helpful ways Pastor Canals shows you how to memorize a text during one week, and, ultimately, memorize entire chapters and books of the Bible, such as Galatians, Ephesians, or Philippians. He helps you realize that your mind can be blessed by the Holy Spirit helping you to memorize and use your mental capacity. He says, "The Holy Spirit is the only one who can help us receive, retain, and reproduce the Word of God when we need it the most. Unless we can store and recall the Word of God, no knowledge of God can be acquired. This is why remembering is so crucial for the children of God."

There are many important reasons to memorize Scripture, including these wonderful reasons given by Pastor Canals: (1) strengthens our faith in God; (2) is a powerful weapon in our spiritual warfare; (3) guides us to make right decisions; (4) prepares us to witness for Christ; (5) energizes and sharpens our minds; (6) allows the Holy Spirit to remind us of the promises of God; and (7) helps us develop the character of Jesus.

He even gives seven very practical daily recommendations and elaborates on them, helping you to be smarter: (1) handwriting the Bible; (2) getting exercise; (3) memorizing the Word of God; (4) drinking plenty of water; (5) eating a simple plant-based diet; (6) getting enough sleep; and (7) exercising self-discipline.

You will be blessed as you read this book, become focused on the Bible, and start memorizing the precious Word of God. God will use you and memorized scriptures to His glory and your spiritual growth. What a privilege to have God's Word to read, study, and place in our hearts through memorization for eternity. By God's grace, get started!

Ted N. C. Wilson
President
General Conference of Seventh-day Adventists

ENDORSEMENTS

"Back to the Bible *is a book born out of the author's experience. That's what makes it so good. It's more than theory. It's the spiritual journey of a changed man. I have had the privilege of working closely with Ramón Canals. I have heard him pray countless times, beautifully intertwining Bible passages with his heartfelt petitions to God. In this book, he shares why and how to memorize Scripture. It is practical, yes. But more than this, every chapter convincingly calls us back to spiritual basics—back to what's important. Above all, this book is hopeful. It reminds us that no matter how far we may be from God, we can still find Him in His Word. We can find His love, forgiveness, and spiritual power. The path is clear. What we need is to get* Back to the Bible."

Jim Howard
Director, Sabbath School and Personal Ministries
Assistant to the President, TMI Lay Training
General Conference of Seventh-day Adventists

"If you truly treasure your Bible and seek the ultimate experience with God's Word, this book is for you. Ramón Canals, while living a dedicated Christian life of service to humanity, has successfully memorized not just a few random verses or chapters, but complete books of the Bible. He writes from experience, his own amazing journey with the sacred Scriptures. Pastor Canals reveals proven practical methods of how an average person can master Bible memorization. But . . . that's just the beginning . . . he shares how an ordinary life can be totally transformed and genuinely blessed when heaven's Word lives in a person's mind and heart."

Anthony R. Kent, Ph.D.
Associate Secretary
Ministerial Association
General Conference of Seventh-day Adventists

"*In* Back to the Bible: A Call to Focus Our Minds on the Word of God, *Ramón Canals reminds us of the central importance of Scripture in personal and spiritual reformation and transformation. He presents an easy-to-follow method for memorizing Scripture as a way to know God's will, follow His plans, and pursue His purposes. It is well worth the read!*"

Dwain N. Esmond
Associate Director
Ellen G. White Estate

"*Something happens in your mind and soul when you slowly place God's Word deep in your heart. The living words in the Bible are a gift from God that draw us close to heaven and change us in ways that nothing else can. In his wonderful book, Pastor Ramón Canals inspires, challenges, and equips us to know how to do this in a very practical way. We need this message at this time—for our children and for ourselves. It's helped me, and I believe it will help you, too.*"

Nina Atcheson, Ped.D. h.c., M.R.E.
Alive in Jesus Curriculum Manager / Senior Editor
Sabbath School and Personal Ministries Department
General Conference of Seventh-day Adventists

Contents

The Unopened Gift That Transformed My Life

"I keep my eyes always on the Lord.
With him at my right hand, I will not be shaken."
—Psalm 16:8

Have you ever received a gift but forgot to open it? Over the years I have received many beautiful gifts from family and friends that I eagerly opened. However, one gift stands out above all others: my first Bible. Although it was the best gift that I had ever received, it was several years before I opened it. The dedication in the Bible read "So that you will never forget your friend or God." This copy of the Bible was given to me by a friend. Unfortunately, with time I had forgotten about my friend and, worse, the God depicted in its pages.

For many years that Bible remained out of view, hidden from the sight of all who lived in my house. This precious book gathered dust; it had no power in my life because it lay buried amid worthless objects. But a miracle occurred early one morning as I was driving back home from a dance hall in New York City. God spoke to me. I heard His voice three times. He told me, *Read the Bible. Read the Bible. Read the Bible.*

Read the Bible? I have never done that in my life, I thought. But that touch of the Almighty could not have come at a more appropriate time. I felt sad, tired, and miserable. I felt like escaping life, especially my youth. Past events made me reflect on the kind of life I was living. Two of my friends had died: one had jumped from the thirty-fifth floor of a building in New York City; the other was stabbed while negotiating a drug deal.

I had just left the dance hall at 4:00 in the morning. And the voice persisted: *Read the Bible. Read the Bible. Read the Bible.* It was not an audible voice, but the impression was so clear that I did not doubt that it was the voice of God.

After getting home, I began reading my Bible. At first I did not understand it, but just reading it brought peace to my heart. Since the day I discovered the Bible, it has been a guiding light in my life.

However, simply owning a Bible is not enough. The devil knows this; therefore, he tries to prevent people from reading and memorizing the Word of God. He doesn't mind you having multiple Bibles as long as you don't let their message be planted in your heart.

We are engaged in a battle for our minds, and the Bible is the primary weapon that can lead us to victory. However, a 2022 report by the American Bible Society revealed that only 10 percent of adult Christians in the United States read the Bible daily.[1] The percentage of Christians reading their Bibles varies from country to country. However, studies show that there has been a consistent decline in Bible reading among Christians. That is why we must continue calling God's people back to the Bible.

FINDING GOD IN SILENT TIMES

Finding unhurried time to connect with God can be difficult in our fast-paced existence. We are often conditioned to be busy constantly. The pressures of modern life can consume every moment, leaving us with little time to cultivate our relationship with God. Finding unrushed time with God has always been my struggle (and I suspect I am not alone). There are times in my Christian experience that I spend hours in communion with God—basking in His presence and immersed in the Word and in prayer. But then I get so busy again that sometimes I scarcely have time to utter a prayer during the whole day.

I am unsatisfied with that type of spiritual life; you should be too. God's Word calls us to focus our eyes on Him always, even when we're busy. Though God desires a personal and intimate relationship with us, we often respond with excuses: too busy, too tired, blah, blah, blah. But the Word of God reminds us gently to be still and know that He is God (Psalm 46:10), and to do that takes time.

God speaks to us in silence, but we are so accustomed to noise and busyness that to be silent seems like a waste of time. However, during these moments of silence, we can hear God's voice calling us to pray and meditate on His Word. He calls us to focus on the Word of God. He is calling us to an intimate relationship with Him. Such a relationship requires stillness and quietness to nurture.

Silence is the environment God designed for us to connect with Him. Ellen G. White wrote, "An intensity such as never before was seen is taking possession of the world. In amusement, in money-making, in the contest for power, in the very struggle for existence, there is a terrible force that engrosses body and mind and soul. In the midst of this maddening rush, God is speaking. He bids us come apart and commune with Him. 'Be still, and know that I am God.' Psalm 46:10."[2]

I was struck by the statement "Many, even in their seasons of devotion, fail of receiving the blessing of real communion with God. They are in too great haste. With hurried steps they press through the circle of Christ's loving presence, pausing perhaps a moment within the sacred precincts, but not waiting for counsel. They have no time to remain with the divine Teacher. With their burdens, they return to their work. These workers can never attain the highest success until they learn the secret of strength. They must give themselves time to think, to pray, to wait upon God for a renewal of physical, mental, and spiritual power. They need the uplifting influence of His Spirit. Receiving this, they will be quickened by fresh life. The wearied frame and tired brain will be refreshed, the burdened heart will be lightened. Not a pause for a moment in His presence, but personal contact with Christ, to sit down in companionship with Him—this is our need."[3]

We are busy, extremely so. Nevertheless, God loves us so much that He desires to draw us closer to Him, and we can do so by spending quiet moments reading, learning, and meditating on His Word. We cannot know God if we are unfamiliar with His Word. Only by studying and learning His Word can we know Him. Memorizing the Word of God is not merely a mechanical exercise of rote learning and repetition; it is about allowing His Word to fill our hearts and minds so that we can always focus on Jesus.

Throughout the history of Christianity, humans have recognized the Bible's transforming power. The power is found, not in the book itself (for it is only ink and paper), but in its content: the living Word of the living God. Perhaps that's why the Lord Jesus said, "Man shall not live on bread alone, but on every word that comes from the mouth of God" (Matthew 4:4).

ANYONE CAN MEMORIZE A BOOK OF THE BIBLE

The Bible has a transforming power that few recognize. My love for the Bible has been profound and deeply personal. When presented with a unique academic challenge during my university years—the memorization of 100 Bible verses—I relished the task.

This endeavor became a pilgrimage of sorts, with each verse carved into the corners of my mind like a sculptor etching intricate patterns onto stone. The journey was undeniably arduous at the onset. Yet as I braved the steep learning curve, it gradually became more manageable. This was the first step in my remarkable foray into Bible memorization. I began to etch entire psalms, key passages, and extensive sections of Scripture into my memory.

Despite my growing cache of memorized verses, I had never tried to commit an entire book of the Bible to memory. Perhaps this was because of a lack of ambition or determination. However, an unexpected hurdle transformed my approach to Scripture memorization.

In 2009 I underwent eye surgery to correct my nearsightedness. However, the surgery significantly impaired my ability to read, and I began to have trouble reading. A few months after my eye surgery I was invited to spearhead a large-scale satellite evangelistic meeting. I wrestled with a predicament: how to read my Bible or even the words on the screen during the meetings.

The idea ignited a passion within me. I made a commitment to memorize word-for-word each biblical verse that I planned to use every night. I prayed to God for help, and He kindly answered my prayers. Every night, as I encouraged the congregation to follow along with verses such as Romans 6:23, I recited the text from memory. Although many people thought I was reading the Bible directly, I had memorized the verses. After successfully reciting the Bible verses without making a mistake for nine consecutive days, I realized the powerful impact of speaking God's Word from memory.

This experience taught me a valuable lesson. With God's help, anyone can memorize many sections of Scripture, perhaps even a whole book of the Bible, and be immensely blessed, just as I have been. This has become my goal. Just imagine the profound power of having the entire Bible committed to memory.

THE PURPOSE OF THE BOOK

This book introduces a simple biblical methodology to help readers rediscover the joy of memorizing the Word of God. I am excited to share the method that helped me to achieve this incredible feat. Imagine committing to memorize one verse every day. By the end of the year, you will have memorized 365 verses, equivalent to more than three books of the Bible—Ephesians, Philippians, and Colossians. If you continue practicing this habit for several years, you can memorize many biblical books. Back to the Bible guides anyone interested in embarking on this transformative journey.

In addition, by committing the Bible to memory, you will uncover the unrivaled method to fortify your faith and strengthen your mental capacity. Committing the Word of God to memory mirrors how we learn a new language. Except that this language is the language of heaven. As the apostle Paul said: "Let the word of Christ dwell in you richly in all wisdom, teaching and admonishing one another in psalms and hymns and spiritual songs, singing with grace in your hearts to the Lord" (Colossians

3:16, NKJV). May God give us hunger for the Word of God, to read it, study it, meditate on it, and share it every day of our lives.

WHY READ THIS BOOK?

This book is intended for those who want to learn more about God's Word; it is also for Christians tired of a routine, monotonous, and robotic religious experience and who crave an authentic, intimate, and close relationship with Jesus. It's for those who want more of His Holy Spirit and are committed to following Jesus. "If you abide in Me, and My words abide in you, you will ask what you desire, and it shall be done for you" (John 15:7, NKJV).

God is calling you and me to focus our hearts and minds on Jesus and His Word. Allowing the Word of God to dwell within us brings us the greatest joy in life. This book will guide you to an exciting spiritual experience with Jesus, leading you back to the altar of prayer and communion with God through His Word.

ENDNOTES

[1] Jeffery Fulks, Randy Petersen, and John Farquhar Plake, *State of the Bible USA 2022* (Philadelphia: American Bible Society, 2022), p. 17.

[2] Ellen G. White, *Education* (Mountain View, Calif.: Pacific Press Pub. Assn., 1903), p. 260.

[3] *Ibid.*, pp. 260, 261.

Chapter 1

The Secret to Memorizing the Bible

"And these words which I command you today shall be in your heart."
—Deuteronomy 6:6, NKJV

"The Bible was given for practical purposes."
—Ellen G. White, *Selected Messages*, book 1, p. 20.

I was born in a secular environment and didn't have any exposure to the Bible or religious teachings. However, when I felt a calling to read the Bible for the first time at the age of 20, it profoundly impacted me. I wanted to learn as much as I could from the Word of God. As I began to enjoy the Word of God, I wanted to write it in my heart. It was very difficult at first. I prayed to find an easier way. I asked God to show me the secret of Bible memorization.

In the book of Deuteronomy God gives us a methodology for learning and memorizing His Word. In Deuteronomy 6 God instructs Moses to teach the people of Israel about His commandments, decrees, and laws, "that you may fear the Lord your God, to keep all His statutes and His commandments which I command you, you and your son and your grandson, all the days of your life, and that your days may be prolonged" (verse 2, NKJV). The reason for this was threefold. To help the people of Israel

(1) learn to fear (reverence) the Lord.

(2) obey His commandments.

(3) live a long life.

The Bible repeats this goal throughout its pages. But the question is *How will people be able to keep His commandments?* Verse 6 provides the answer: "These commandments that I give you today are to be on your hearts." In other words, these commandments must be received and kept in the heart. God wants His children to obey His commandments, but to do that, He placed a commandment within the commandments that tells them how to follow the law. And the only way to do that is by keeping the Word of God in their hearts.

In this chapter you find seven verbs that help in this process:

1. **Teach**—Teaching includes learning and sharing.
   Teach others about God's Word and instructions.
2. **Observe**—Pay attention, understand, and make a
   conscious decision to live accordingly.
3. **Obey**—Put into practice what you have learned.
4. **Impress**—Repeat the verse over and over until it is
   impressed in the heart.
5. **Talk**—Share the Word of God all that you can.
   Speak about His works and wonders.
6. **Bind**—A strong bonding happens when you dwell on
   Bible verses. They join with your thoughts and are bound
   to you. They become your possession.
7. **Write**—Engrave, record, and register the words in your
   mind and heart.

THE SEVEN-PART SECRET

These seven verbs show that the Word of God was given for memorization. A closer look at them within the context of Deuteronomy will show us that they reveal a secret for memorizing the Bible.

1. TEACH/LEARN: The Hebrew word *lamad* refers to the process of learning and teaching, which happens as we study and internalize Scripture. This is the first step in a lifelong journey of faith. Learning is essential to remembering and applying its teachings in our daily lives.

Ultimately, learning is crucial to our spiritual growth. It enables us to deepen our relationship with God and to live according to His will. This process is important because we remember only what we learn. Interestingly, the same Hebrew root, *lamad*, is used for both learning and teaching. This reflects the Hebrew idea that teaching and learning are deeply interconnected.

Putting God's Word to memory involves more than learning and obeying. We will also share its knowledge, wisdom, and guidance with others. We will help them understand and embrace God's truth. Teaching is crucial to faith. It ensures that religious beliefs and practices are passed on.

2. OBSERVE: In Deuteronomy 6, particularly in the context of the Shema (verses 4-9), the term *observe* is translated from the Hebrew word "שָׁמַר" (*shamar*), which means to keep, guard, observe, give heed. This implies a careful attention and a faithful adherence to the commands, statutes, and laws given by God. It's not merely about passive observation or awareness; it is, instead, an active, diligent commitment to live out the teachings and commandments. We are more alert, watchful, and intent to follow God's will when we memorize Bible passages.

3. OBEY: While "obey" is not directly a Hebrew verb, the closest concept in this context is *shama*, often translated as "hear," or "listen." In Hebrew thought, listening is closely linked to obeying because to truly hear is to act upon what is heard. Thus, *shama* would imply not only hearing God's Word but putting it into practice. It's more than head knowledge or understanding. Obedience means living according to God's laws and commands, showing a commitment to His principles in actions and decisions.

4. IMPRESS: Repeat a verse over and over until it leaves its mark in the heart. We teach the Word to ourselves, and to others, in order to ensure that it is deeply ingrained and constantly recalled. This is crucial for making the teachings part of our nature. The idea of repetition here is tied to deeply fixing God's Word in one's heart. It suggests a continuous and persistent reflection on the Scriptures. This constant engagement with the text ensures that it becomes a part of our inner being and, therefore, influences our thoughts and actions.

5. TALK: Speak about God's laws and principles; share His teachings in everyday life. We keep the Word of God active in our speech and interactions. We can do this in various settings—within the family, among friends, and in the community. This constant verbalization of faith helps reinforce its teaching for us, as well as spread the teachings to others.

In Colossians 3:16 the apostle Paul expressed this same idea: "Let the word of Christ dwell in you richly in all wisdom, teaching and admonishing one another in psalms and hymns and spiritual songs, singing with grace in your hearts to the Lord" (NKJV).

6. BIND/TIE: This verb symbolizes creating a strong, enduring connection with God's Word. It suggests an intimate and permanent bonding with the teachings, making them an inseparable part of our life and identity. It is almost as if they are "tied" to our being.

7. WRITE: The Hebrew word for "write" or "inscribe" holds a significant meaning in a religious context. It emphasizes the importance of preserving and documenting the sacred texts. However, it also carries a deeper meaning: engraving. When we etch biblical teaching onto our hearts and minds, they become a constant guiding presence.

The act of writing in this context is not just about putting words on a surface, but rather about imprinting God's Word deeply into our very being. It symbolizes making a permanent mark to ensure that the teachings are remembered and preserved.

LOVE FOR GOD AND HIS WORD

The command to "love God with all our heart" (see Matthew 22:37) is a call to devote ourselves solely and wholeheartedly to

Him. This commandment signifies the importance of unity and demands our undivided loyalty. It's not about loving many things; it's about loving the one true God, who created the heavens and the earth. Love is at the core of God's nature, and everything originates from Him. As God's children, we should embody His character by filling ourselves with His love. This love will overflow from our hearts and be spread to others around us.

God's commandment instructs you and me to love completely and wholeheartedly. This means dedicating our entire being— heart, mind, and soul—to loving God. It's an all-encompassing commitment that leaves no room for half measures. Loving God with all our soul means involving every part of our being, while loving with all our strength requires us to dedicate our entire capacity to this love. This complete surrender to God is a call to turn wholly toward the One we love.

How can we achieve such a level of surrender and love toward God, the Creator of the universe? God gives us the answer through His Word. He encourages us to engage deeply with His teachings—learning, observing, obeying, repeating, talking about, and internalizing the words in the Bible. This isn't a casual engagement, but a deep and persistent one. Repetition creates habit, which in turn becomes part of our being. As these teachings become ingrained in us, our character transforms and becomes more aligned with God's character.

It is essential to surrender ourselves entirely to His will. Only then can we truly live out the commandment to love God with all our heart, soul, and strength and to experience a significant transformation.

God commands parents to teach His laws to their children. However, it's impossible to teach something that we don't know. Therefore, the commandment to teach also includes a commandment to learn. Moreover, the commandment to teach and learn is also a call to put God's laws into practice and obey them.

REPETITION: THE SECRET CODE

When we repeat something daily, it becomes a habit. By repeating the words of God each day, the people of Israel would have His words engraved in their minds. These words would help them develop the habit of obeying God, a transformation of character that would reflect God's character. So what is a habit? A habit is a deliberate decision that we make in our lives, which we practice daily until it becomes automatic. This is the secret code for memorizing the Word of God.

God intended for His people to develop the habit of having His Word in their hearts. I call this the secret of Bible memorization, not because it is hidden, but because few people have discovered the power of living a life, according to Deuteronomy 6.

Listen to these words from Deuteronomy 6:7-9:

1. **"Impress them on your children"** all the time!

2. **"Talk about them when you sit at home"** anytime.

3. **"Talk about them . . . when you walk along the road"** during the day.

4. **"Talk about them . . . when you lie down"** at night.

5. **"Talk about them . . . when you get up"** in the morning.

6. **"Tie them as symbols on your hands"** daily.

7. **"Bind them on your foreheads"** daily.

8. **"Write them on the doorframes of your houses"** daily.

9. **"Write them . . . on your gates"** daily.

This sounds like total saturation in the Word of God. It is basking in the Word, which in turn is basking in God's presence.

In her book *As Light Lingers: Basking in the Word of God*, Nina Atcheson writes, "The words sit there on the pages of your Bible, but how can you keep God's Word in your heart? We can start by putting them there in an intentional way. 'Your word I have hidden in my heart,' David said, 'that I might not sin against You' (Psalm 119:11, NKJV). I mean keeping God's words in our hearts, where we have easy access to them."[1]

Atcheson shares a simple, practical, and very insightful method of studying the Bible:[2]

The Verse-by-Verse Method

1. Ask Jesus to be with you as you read.
2. Choose a Bible verse or passage.
3. Write the passage into your journal. Then read it aloud.
4. Underline the big idea in the passage.
5. Write down what this big idea tells you about God or yourself.
6. Write down (or whisper) a prayer of what you want to say to Jesus.

Word Study

The steps are as follows:

1. Pray for the Holy Spirit to guide your mind and heart as you read.
2. Write out the same verse multiple times.
3. Consider the different words in the verse.
4. Write down your thoughts about what these words are saying to you today.
5. Write a prayer response to God.

This is a simple yet profound method of studying and learning the Bible. Atcheson points out, "You can see how powerful it is to meditate on a small portion of God's Word. God has spoken truth into my soul on many occasions through this method of simply and prayerfully considering one verse and what that verse speaks into my life that morning. You can see how simple it is to consider the meaning, word by word, and to respond to the verse upon conclusion."[3]

God wants His people to learn His commands, decrees, and laws because He wants to bless them with a wonderful, happy, and long life. As parents we want the best for our children. How much more God our Father wants the best for us, His children. But we cannot compare ourselves with our amazing God and amazing Father. This is why Jesus says, "If you then, though you are evil, know how to give good gifts to your children, how much more will your Father in heaven give the Holy Spirit to those who ask Him!" (Luke 11:13).

God is such a loving and wonderful God that He wants to bless His children with every spiritual blessing in the heavenly places. Because He loves you and wants to bless you, He says, "Observe and obey all these words which I command you, that it may go well with you and your children after you forever" (Deuteronomy 12:28, NKJV). Loving obedience to God is the result of knowing God. The more we know God, the more we want to obey. We obey because we love Him. Obedience, therefore, is not a burden but a pleasure.

Those who learn the Word of God by memory will know the heart of God and will want to obey Him with all their hearts. Jesus says that eternal life is to know God (John 17:3). And those who memorize the Word of God will have the privilege of knowing God and His will for humanity.

ONE FOCUS

The human mind has a limitation—it can focus on only one thing at a time. The human mind cannot occupy two thoughts simultaneously. That is why Jesus said in Matthew 6:24: "No one can serve two masters. Either you will hate the one and love the other, or you will be devoted to the one and despise the other. You cannot serve both God and money." This is about focus. It is about commitment. It is about total surrendering of our lives to God.

Moses, a man who talked with God and saw His glory, admonished people o love God with all their heart, soul, and strength (Deuteronomy 6:5). Because God is our Creator, He knows our weaknesses. He knows how our brain works. He knows we cannot pay attention to two things simultaneously, and can focus only on one thing at a time. That is why He says in Deuteronomy 6:4: "Hear, O Israel: The Lord our God, the Lord is one." Therefore, love One, serve One, obey One, and worship One—the Creator of the universe. This is the message of the three angels of Revelation 14.

The methodology Deuteronomy 6 presents for fixing the Word of God in our hearts and minds is designed to help us fulfill the command to pray without ceasing. God, through Moses, provides a framework for implanting His Word into our hearts. This chapter highlights how we can integrate this command of God into all aspects of daily life.

Deuteronomy 6 starts with the command to love God with all our heart, soul, and strength (verse 5). This command suggests a form of continuous devotion and focus on God, a foundational aspect of unceasing prayer. Verses 6-9 in this chapter instruct us to:

➤ Keep these words in their heart.

➤ Teach them to their children.

➤ Talk about them at home and on the road.

➤ Bind them as symbols on their hands and foreheads.

This constant engagement with God's Word throughout the day, in all settings and actions, can also be seen as a form of continuous, living prayer.

Deuteronomy 6 also reminds us of God's acts and the importance of keeping His commands to respond to His faithfulness (verses 10-12). Remembering and recounting God's deeds and blessings can be a form of prayer that acknowledges and honors God continually.

The chapter concludes with an emphasis on fearing God and obeying all His commandments (verses 13-25). Respecting and adhering to God's commands is a form of ongoing spiritual discipline and can be interpreted as a prayerful way of life.

Deuteronomy 6 outlines a plan for integrating God's commandments into everyday life. This involves cultivating a continuous state of prayer through love, remembrance, instruction, and obedience to God. This approach aligns with the idea of praying without ceasing, as it involves making every aspect of our lives an expression of devotion.

The commandment to love God with all our heart, soul, and strength is a divine order. It calls us to focus solely on God and eliminate anything that may divert our attention from Him. All our love and strength must be directed toward God. We learn and practice this commandment because we love God.

ACTION STEPS

What changes can you make today to love God with all your heart, soul, and strength?

1. What are the steps you can take today to help you learn, obey, teach, repeat, talk, bind, and write the Word of God in your heart?

2. What are the things that distract you from loving God with all your heart?

3. What three decisions you make today will strengthen your relationship with God?

ENDNOTES

[1]Nina Atcheson, *As Light Lingers: Basking in the Word of God* (Madrid: Editorial Safeliz, 2018), p. 34.

[2]*Ibid.*, p. 71.

[3]*Ibid.*, p. 73.

Chapter II

The Key to Bible Memorization

"But the Helper, the Holy Spirit,
whom the Father will send in My name,
He will teach you all things,
and bring to your remembrance
all things that I said to you."
—John 14:26, NKJV

I used to struggle to be able to pray for more than a few minutes at a time, which bothered me. I wanted to pray for hours, as Jesus did. The more I tried, the more difficult it became. My mind was always wandering. I could not stay focused. It was frustrating. However, everything changed when I started memorizing the Bible and asking the Holy Spirit to help me remember it. Now I can pray focused for a long time because the Holy Spirit helps me to remember God's words. Praying back Bible verses is an excellent way to remember them and to think deeply about their meaning.

This method turned my prayer life around. Before, I felt stuck and disappointed because I couldn't pray long. But learning the Bible by heart opened a whole new way to talk to God. Now when I pray, I use the words from the Bible, and it feels as if I have endless things to say. It's like having a conversation in which God's words guide me. This way, my prayers feel more meaningful and powerful.

I also noticed that praying with the Bible's words aligns my prayers more with the will of God. Instead of just asking for things, I'm now praising, thanking, and asking based on what I've learned from the Scriptures. I feel closer to God because I'm using His words to talk to Him. Memorizing the Bible not only improved my ability to pray for a longer time but also deepened my relationship with God. It's a practice I recommend to anyone who wants to grow in their faith and prayer life.

For many years I prayed, "God, please show me a simple way to memorize the Bible and teach it to others." I read many books and learned a lot of methods for memorization. However, I was not satisfied with the results. The strategies I learned seemed dry, cumbersome, mechanical. They were missing something. I learned some books of the Bible, but afterward I quickly forgot them. For example, I memorized the book of Revelation. But, after great effort, I could recall only a few chapters. So I continued to seek a more effective and simpler way.

OUR HELPER

I knew that memorizing was hard. But I was willing to pay the price. I was not trying to find an easy method. I was already determined to memorize Bible books, no matter what I had to do. I loved it. And this is my passion. However, I wanted to find a simple approach to teach others to do the same. I wanted to share with others the blessings that I received daily in my walk with God, allowing Him to write His Word on my heart.

So I kept praying until God put the thought in my mind. It was a Bible verse: "But the Helper, the Holy Spirit, whom the Father will send in My name, He will teach you all things, and bring to your remembrance all things that I said to you" (John 14:26, NKJV). Jesus said, *The Holy Spirit will remind you of My words.* That was it!

The key to memorizing the Word of God is the Holy Spirit. It makes sense because it was the Holy Spirit who inspired the authors of the Bible to write the Word of God. The Bible says, "All Scripture is given by inspiration of God, and is profitable for doctrine, for reproof, for correction, for instruction in righteousness, that the man of God may be complete, thoroughly equipped for every good work" (2 Timothy 3:16, 17, NKJV). The Holy Spirit is the inspiration of the Scriptures. And the Holy Spirit illuminates the mind of anyone with a burning desire to know the Word of God. He will help you learn it. He will help you understand it. And He will help you remember the Word of God.

Ellen G. White says, "God will flash the knowledge obtained by diligent searching of the Scriptures, into their memory at the very time when it is needed. But if they neglect to fill their minds with the gems of truth, if they do not acquaint themselves with the words of Christ, if they have never tasted the power of His grace in trial, then they cannot expect that the Holy Spirit will bring His words to their remembrance. They are to serve God daily with their undivided affections, and then trust Him."[1]

JESUS, OUR EXAMPLE

Jesus Christ is our ultimate role model in every aspect of life. From the moment He was born, to His death, resurrection, and ascension, He was guided by the Holy Spirit. One of the most important examples he set for us was His knowledge of the Bible. He knew the Scriptures by heart, which is evident from His ministry. The New Testament contains several instances in which Jesus Christ was guided by the Holy Spirit and demonstrated an intimate familiarity with the Scriptures. These texts indicate His life was guided by the Holy Spirit: Luke 1:35; Luke 2:25-38; Matthew 3:16, 17; Luke 4:1, 2, 14-21; Matthew 12:28; John 14:15-17, 26; Hebrews 9:14; Romans 8:11; Acts 1:8; Acts 2:1-4.

These Old Testament texts indicate His vast knowledge of the Scriptures.

- ➢ **Genesis 2:24**: Quoted in Matthew 19:5; Mark 10:7, 8; Ephesians 5:31.

- ➢ **Exodus 20:12-16; Deuteronomy 5:16-20**: Quoted in Matthew 19:18, 19.

- ➢ **Exodus 3:6**: Quoted in Matthew 22:32; Mark 12:26; Luke 20:37.

- ➢ **Leviticus 19:18**: Quoted in Matthew 19:19; Matthew 22:39; Mark 12:31; Luke 10:27.

- ➢ **Deuteronomy 6:16**: Quoted in Matthew 4:7; Luke 4:12.

➢ **Deuteronomy 6:5**: Quoted in Matthew 22:37; Mark 12:30; Luke 10:27.

➢ **Psalm 110:1**: Quoted in Matthew 22:44; Mark 12:36; Luke 20:42, 43; Acts 2:34, 35.

➢ **Psalm 118:22, 23**: Quoted in Matthew 21:42; Mark 12:10, 11; Luke 20:17.

➢ **Psalm 8:2**: Quoted in Matthew 21:16.

➢ **Psalm 82:6**: Quoted in John 10:34.

➢ **Psalm 22**: Alluded to in Matthew 27:46; Mark 15:34.

➢ **Isaiah 6:9, 10**: Quoted in Matthew 13:14, 15, Mark 4:12, Luke 8:10.

➢ **Isaiah 29:13**: Quoted in Matthew 15:8, 9; Mark 7:6, 7.

➢ **Jeremiah 7:11**: Quoted in Matthew 21:13; Mark 11:17; Luke 19:46.

➢ **Daniel 7:13, 14**: Alluded to in Matthew 24:30; Mark 13:26; Luke 21:27.

➢ **Micah 6:8**: Alluded to in Matthew 23:23.

➢ **Hosea 6:6**: Quoted in Matthew 9:13; 12:7.

➢ **Jonah 1:17**: Alluded to in Matthew 12:40.

➢ **Malachi 3:1**: Quoted in Matthew 11:10, Mark 1:2, Luke 7:27.

Jesus' life and ministry were deeply rooted in the Scriptures. His ability to recall, interpret, and fulfill the Scriptures highlights His identity as the Word made flesh (John 1:14). Jesus' example inspires us to turn back to the Bible, to seek spiritual understanding from the text, and to put our lives in harmony with the Scriptures. There is no better way to do this than by consciously and intentionally allowing the Word of God to dwell in our hearts and change our lives.

THE DISCIPLES OF JESUS

Jesus' disciples had an exceptional understanding of the Scriptures. After receiving the Holy Spirit at Pentecost (Acts 2), they demonstrated, by their teachings and preaching, a profound knowledge of the Scriptures. They frequently referred to the Hebrew Scriptures. Two examples are Peter's sermon at Pentecost (Acts 2:14-36) and Stephen's speech before the Sanhedrin (Acts 7). Both accounts reveal their deep familiarity with the Word of God.

In the Jewish culture of the first century A.D., teachings were often passed down through oral tradition. The disciples may not have needed to memorize the Scriptures entirely. But their ability to recall and apply scriptural teachings in different contexts indicates a strong familiarity with the key themes and passages of the Scriptures.

In His teachings Jesus often used references to the Hebrew Scriptures. As His primary audience, the disciples would have had many opportunities to learn and to internalize these Scriptures through His interpretation and application. The New Testament records that after His resurrection Jesus "opened their minds so they could understand the Scriptures" (Luke 24:45). This suggests that their grasp of the Scriptures was significantly deepened and enlightened by Jesus Himself. Though the New Testament does not explicitly teach that all of them knew the Bible by heart, their ability to effectively use and interpret the Scriptures speaks to their deep understanding.

THE WALDENSIANS

The Waldensians were a Christian movement that began in the twelfth century A.D. The group originated with Peter Waldo, a wealthy merchant from Lyon, France. The Waldensians had a particularly significant relationship with the Bible, which was central to their beliefs and practices. Memorization of the Bible was crucial to them. This aspect of their religious practice was both a spiritual discipline and a practical necessity because of the circumstances of the time.

In the time of the Waldensians, access to written texts was limited and controlled, so they had to memorize huge portions of the Bible. This innovative approach was integral to their identity as a movement, which was focused on a return to the basics of Christian doctrine and lifestyle.

Ellen G. White wrote about the Waldensians. "Pure, simple, and fervent was the piety of these followers of Christ. The principles of truth they valued above houses and lands, friends, kindred, even life itself. These principles they earnestly sought to impress upon the hearts of the young. From earliest childhood the youth were instructed in the Scriptures and taught to regard sacredly the claims of the law of God. Copies of the Bible were rare; therefore, its precious words were committed to memory. Many were able to repeat large portions of both the Old and the New Testament. Thoughts of God were associated alike with the sublime scenery of nature and with the humble blessings of daily life. Little children learned to look with gratitude to God as the giver of every favor and every comfort. . . .

"From their pastors the youth received instruction. While attention was given to branches of general learning, the Bible was made the chief study. The Gospels of Matthew and John were committed to memory, with many of the Epistles. They were employed also in copying the Scriptures. Some manuscripts contained the whole Bible, others only brief selections, to which some simple explanations of the text were added by those who were able to expound the Scriptures. Thus were brought forth the treasures of truth so long concealed by those who sought to exalt themselves above God."[2]

THE PIONEERS OF THE CHURCH

John Nevins Andrews was a pioneer Seventh-day Adventist scholar, author, and the first American Adventist minister sent overseas. He developed deep religious convictions at a very early age. However, because of health reasons, he had to leave school at age 11. Despite this disadvantage, he continued to read books and educate himself while working on his father's farm. He found the Savior at age 13 and devoted himself to the Advent Awakening, which swept the world in the 1830s and 1840s.

Andrews always rose at 4:00 in the morning and spent two or three hours studying the Bible and praying before breakfast. His love for the Bible led him to center his intellectual pursuits on it. On his own, one by one, he mastered Greek, Latin, and Hebrew so that he could study God's Word in the original languages.

Near the end of his life, rumors circulated that he had memorized the entire Bible. A friend ventured, "I hear you can repeat the whole Bible from memory." He smiled. "So far as the New Testament is concerned, if it were obliterated, I could reproduce it word for word; but I could not say as much for the Old Testament." His stature as a scholar, writer, and minister may be largely attributed to his hard study, earnest prayer, and deep commitment to Christ.

YOU, TOO

You may think memorizing the Bible is a good idea, but not for you. You have probably convinced yourself that you have a lousy memory. You cannot recall anything, and therefore this idea will not work for you. But what if it is not about your memory capacity but about the Holy Spirit helping you memorize? Additionally, experts in memory training assert that there is no such thing as a bad or good memory. It is about a trained or untrained memory.

On this point Ellen G. White says, "The mind must be restrained, and not allowed to wander. It should be trained to dwell upon the Scriptures; even whole chapters may be committed to memory, to be repeated when Satan comes in with his temptations. The fifty-eighth of Isaiah is a profitable chapter for this purpose. Wall the soul in with the restrictions and instructions given by the inspiration of the Spirit of God. When Satan would lead the mind to dwell upon earthly and sensual things, he is most effectually resisted with 'It is written.' When he suggests doubts as to whether we are really the people whom God is leading, whom by tests and provings he is preparing to stand in the great day, be ready to meet his insinuations by presenting the clear evidence from the Word of God that we are keeping the commandments of God and the faith of Jesus."[3]

The Holy Spirit inspired the authors of Scripture to write it. That is why He is the key to Bible memorization. "But the Helper, the Holy Spirit, whom the Father will send in My name, He will teach you all things, and bring to your remembrance all things that I said to you" (John 14:26, NKJV).

The Holy Spirit is the only one who can help us receive, retain, and reproduce the Word of God when we need it the most. Unless we can store and recall the Word of God, no knowledge of God can be acquired. This is why remembering is so crucial for the children of God.

35

The people of Israel are a perfect example of how easy it is to forget God. Though having experienced miracles and wonders for many years, they soon forgot God and went their own way, even to the point of worshipping false gods. By constantly meditating on the Word of God, we have the opportunity and privilege of turning our eyes upon Jesus and setting our hearts and minds on the things above, where Jesus is ministering on our behalf.

By storing the Word of God in our minds, we learn how to be godly people. Wickedness brought on the destruction of the earth. "Then the Lord saw that the wickedness of man was great in the earth, and that every intent of the thoughts of his heart was only evil continually" (Genesis 6:5, NKJV).

Godly thinking is not automatic. Our minds are used to negative, worldly, and sinful thinking. We are advised to set our hearts and minds on the things above, where Christ Jesus is sitting at the right hand of God (Colossians 3:1). We are encouraged to think about the things of heaven, and not the earthly things. But can we do that when we are so used to focusing on the things here? We can achieve this only by the grace of God and only by the power and guidance of the Holy Spirit.

ACTION STEPS

1. Ask God for a fresh baptism of the Holy Spirit every day.

2. Ask the Holy Spirit to teach you Christ's words and to help you remember them.

3. Believe that the Holy Spirit has descended upon you and is now guiding you.

ENDNOTES

[1] Ellen G. White, *Counsels on Sabbath School Work* (Washington, D.C.: Review and Herald Pub. Assn., 1938), p. 41.
[2] Ellen G. White, *The Great Controversy* (Mountain View, Calif.: Pacific Press Pub. Assn., 1911), pp. 67-69.
[3] Ellen G. White, *Gospel Workers* (Battle Creek, Mich.: Review and Herald Pub. Co., 1892), p. 418.

Chapter III
Why Memorize the Word?

*"This Book of the Law shall not depart from your mouth, but
you shall meditate in it day and night, that you may observe to
do according to all that is written in it. For then you will make
your way prosperous, and then you will have good success."*
—Joshua 1:8, NKJV

Several years ago a woman possessed by an evil spirit called
my house: "Pastor, please come and help me!"

"Maria, Maria, what's happening to you?" I asked.

Maria did not respond. Suddenly a man's voice, sharp and chill-
ing, and amid his mocking laughter, replied, "You cannot help her;
she belongs to me."

I immediately realized that I was dealing with a supernatural
power. I tried to rebuke the demon with my limited experience
with helping people possessed by evil spirits, but it just laughed at
me more eagerly. Maria kept pleading, "Please help me, help me!"

I had never felt, as I did at that moment, such a need to seek
God and to prepare my heart. I was terrified of facing that demon.
My knees were shaking. Then I remembered the biblical text that
says, "If you have faith as a mustard seed, . . . nothing will be impossible for you" (Matthew 17:20, NKJV).

I prayed for more than an hour and then went to the home of
that poor woman, whom the demon had been harassing for more
than 30 years. Before I got out of the car, I prayed again: "Please

help me. Make that evil spirit go away." Matthew 17:20 came back to my mind: "If you have faith as a mustard seed, . . . nothing will be impossible for you."

That Bible text strengthened my faith. I felt the encouraging presence of Jesus. The fear that had overwhelmed me had disappeared. No more fear. He who said, "I am with you alway, even unto the end of the world" (Matthew 28:20, KJV), was present.

Thanks to Jesus, when I entered the house, I felt the power of God and rebuked the demon. After throwing the woman to the floor, the demon left her. She was motionless, lying on the floor with her eyes closed as if sleeping. Then I called her name: "Maria, Maria." She woke up disoriented and had no clue about what had happened. The power of Jesus freed Maria.

This incident has encouraged me to keep learning Bible promises by heart in order to use in spiritual warfare. I realize, as Paul says, that our struggle is not with one another, but with spiritual forces. "Finally, my brethren, be strong in the Lord and in the power of His might. Put on the whole armor of God, that you may be able to stand against the wiles of the devil. For we do not wrestle against flesh and blood, but against principalities, against powers, against the rulers of the darkness of this age, against spiritual hosts of wickedness in the heavenly places" (Ephesians 6:10-12, NKJV).

Many people, when they were children, may have participated in contests in which they had to memorize Bible verses or even a whole book of the Bible. It may have seemed challenging and tedious at the time. Yet we must remember the life-changing power of memorizing the Scriptures. In fact, for a disciple of Jesus Christ, there is nothing more exciting than learning the Bible.

At first, memorizing may seem complicated and exacting, but it becomes easier and enjoyable with practice. Ellen G. White wrote, "The minds of all who make the Word of God their study will enlarge. Far more than any other study its influence is calculated to increase the powers of comprehension and endow every faculty with new power. It brings the mind in contact with broad, ennobling principles of truth. It brings all heaven into close connection with human minds, imparting wisdom and knowledge and understanding."[1]

Memorizing the Bible expands our minds, enhances our understanding, and allows us to glorify God. We have been given powerful brains, and there is no better way to use them than to memorize God's Word and keep it close to our hearts. We don't need any other reason to memorize the Bible other than that it is the Word of God. Still, having a "why" behind our actions can be helpful.

MY JOURNEY TO "WHY"

Without God, I was devoid of hope. I constantly searched for purpose and direction, having tried numerous paths but never finding the fulfillment that I had yearned for. Then one day my friend Andy invited me to church. I went because he was my friend, and I wanted to understand more about God.

At his church I became fascinated by the idea of memorizing the Bible. I had never considered the concept of embedding Scripture into my memory in order to know more about God.

Motivated by this newfound interest, I started with a modest goal: memorize one verse each week. Initially the task was challenging. As I persisted, I noticed the verses that I memorized provided me comfort and strength during tough times. My relationship with God grew stronger as I pondered the Scriptures.

Continuing my journey of memorizing Bible verses, I discovered that I was better able to resist temptation and overcome sin. The words of Psalm 119:9 resonated deeply with me: "How can a young man cleanse his way? By taking heed according to Your word" (NKJV). My spiritual disciplines, including my self-control, were improving. I felt myself growing in wisdom and gaining a deeper understanding of God's ways, which enabled me to better share the gospel with others.

Eventually I memorized an entire chapter of the Bible. It filled me with a sense of achievement. This journey of learning the Bible had been transformative, bringing me closer to God and enhancing my understanding of His Word.

Committing verses to memory equipped me to better apply the Bible's truths to my life, to share the gospel more effectively, and to stand firmer against temptation and sin. Learning God's Word was a powerful tool in combating the devil.

SETTLING INTO THE WORD

Even though my parents were not religious, my grandmother was devoutly Catholic and used to take me to church often. However, I was never involved in Bible study. After my baptism into the Seventh-day Adventist Church, I was given an assignment that I credit for helping me develop a love for memorizing Bible texts. The church leaders asked me to teach the Sabbath School lesson to the young people.

Although never having studied the Bible before, let alone taught it, I took this responsibility seriously. I began to study the *Adult Bible Study Guides* and the Bible intensely, which included my memorizing key texts. I used to get up very early to study the Bible lessons. One of the reasons I spent so much time studying the Bible was that I knew very little about it. I wanted to be sure that I knew my lesson well before the class on Sabbath.

Getting up early and dedicating hours to prayer and the daily study of the Bible were instrumental in cementing my faith and deepening my love for my Savior, Jesus. I grew spiritually as I spent time with God and His Word. This will be the same result for anyone who spends time with God and the study of His Word. As we grow spiritually, we not only become aware of our fallen condition but are also more willing to become partners with God in saving souls for the kingdom of heaven.

The Word of God is also our weapon against the enemy. Imagine a soldier who goes to battle without weapons. The enemy attacks, but the soldier cannot defend himself. He left his rifle in the barracks, and now he cannot retrieve it, because he is under heavy artillery fire. The situation worsens when he is badly injured and needs medical attention. His fellow soldiers rescue him, but he nearly dies—all because he forgot to bring his weapon to the battlefield.

The Bible tells us that we are at war with the enemy. Paul says in Ephesians 6:12, 13, "For we do not wrestle against flesh and blood, but against principalities, against powers, against the rulers of the darkness of this age, against spiritual hosts of wickedness in the heavenly places. Therefore take up the whole armor of God, that you may be able to withstand in the evil day, and having done all, to stand" (NKJV).

Because we are involved in this great cosmic battle, we must put on the whole armor of God, including "the helmet of salvation, and the sword of the Spirit, which is the word of God" (Ephesians 6:17, NKJV). The Word of God is our defense against the devil. However unbelievable to think of a soldier going to battle without his weapon, many people go about their daily lives oblivious of this spiritual warfare, and utterly unprepared. They neglect to carry the sword of the Spirit, the Word of God, in their hearts, leaving themselves vulnerable to temptations from the enemy.

Memorizing the Bible is a powerful weapon. By committing verses to memory, we can be equipped to resist temptation and overcome sin. Therefore, memorizing the Bible is essential for spiritual survival and growth.

SEVEN REASONS TO MEMORIZE THE BIBLE . . .

REASON 1:

Memorizing the Word of God Strengthens Our Faith in God

The main reason for memorizing the Word of God is to know God. The more we know God, the more we want to trust Him. The more we trust Him, the more we want to please Him in every way, bearing fruit and growing in the knowledge of God.

Jesus said, "And this is life eternal life, that they may know thee the only true God, and Jesus Christ, whom thou hast sent" (John 17:3, KJV). The biblical definition of eternal life is to know God. This knowledge is not just intellectual, but relational. This knowledge implies an intimate relationship with God. When we know God, we learn to love Him because we discover that God is so good and desires the best for us.

David knew God personally and intimately, so he wrote, "O taste and see that the Lord is good: blessed is the man that trusteth in him" (Psalm 34:8, KJV). But how can one know God? Only through His revelation (which includes nature). God revealed Himself to man through the Scriptures in order to show that He is love itself. The Bible reveals His love for humanity,

We can say that we don't need to memorize the Bible; we need only to read it. Yes, we must read it. God wants us to read the Bible and to develop a personal relationship with Him. That is crucial for having a relationship with God. However, we must place the Word of God in our hearts in order go deeper into that relationship.

Although reading the Bible helps us know God, nothing is more effective in maintaining spiritual life than continually keeping the Word of God in mind. Sadly, many Christians are content with having secondhand experiences in their Christian lives. Instead of living a life focused on Jesus and learning from Him, they settle for a borrowed Christian experience. They hear other people's testimonies and experiences and rejoice in those experiences. There is nothing wrong with that. However, we must have our own experience as well. No one can eat for you. In the same way, no one can have an experience with God for you.

Why have a secondhand experience when we can have a first-hand one? Paul had a burning desire to know Christ: "I want to know Christ—yes, to know the power of his resurrection and participation in his sufferings, becoming like him in his death" (Philippians 3:10). Paul is saying here, I gave up everything, all my earthly possessions, to know Christ personally. That should be the goal of every disciple of Christ. There is no better way of achieving this goal than by putting the Word of God in the heart.

Paul considers knowing Jesus better than anything this world has to offer. This is how he puts it: "But whatever were gains to me I now consider loss for the sake of Christ. What is more, I consider everything a loss because of the surpassing worth of knowing Christ Jesus my Lord, for whose sake I have lost all things. I consider them garbage, that I may gain Christ" (Philippians 3:7, 8). Knowing Christ strengthens our faith in God.

Furthermore, faith comes by hearing the Word of God. That is how we appropriate ourselves to the merits of Christ and His righteousness. "So then faith comes by hearing and hearing by the word of God" (Romans 10:17, NKJV). Paul presents the whole salvation experience as one that starts from faith and ends in faith (Romans 1:17).

Ellen G. White wrote, "It is not enough to believe about Christ; we must believe in Him. The only faith that will benefit us is that which embraces Him as a personal Saviour; which appropriates His merits to ourselves."[2] And again: "The faith that is unto salvation is not a casual faith, it is not the mere consent of the intellect, it is belief rooted in the heart, that embraces Christ as a personal Saviour. . . . This faith leads its possessor to place all the affections of the soul upon Christ."[3]

This is the type of faith that we receive when, led by the Holy Spirit, we get into the Word of God. Memorizing the Word of God means constant repetition of it, and meditation on it, which will elevate our daily thoughts to the things above and not on things below.

REASON 2:
Memorizing the Word of God Is a Powerful Weapon in Our Spiritual Warfare

Knowing the Word of God by heart is a powerful weapon to overcome sin. The apostle Paul calls the Word of God the "sword of the Spirit" (Ephesians 6:17). We will have a constant struggle with sin as long as we are in this world.

The devil is a dangerous enemy and seeks to entangle us in sin. Perhaps that's why the psalmist David asks, "How can a young person stay on the path of purity? By living according to your word. I seek you with all my heart; do not let me stray from your commands. I have hidden your word in my heart that I might not sin against you" (Psalm 119:9-11).

Putting the Word of God in our hearts will protect us when the devil tempts us; it will prevent us from slipping. "The law of his God is in his heart; none of his steps shall slide" (Psalm 37:31, NKJV). David is saying here that memorizing the Word of God will be a deterrent against backsliding. Memorizing Scripture is a powerful weapon in our spiritual warfare. During His temptation by Satan, Jesus countered each temptation with quotes from Deuteronomy. Jesus fought the devil with the Scriptures (Matthew 4:1-11).

When I confronted the woman who was possessed by an evil spirit, I was unsure of what to do. I relied on my knowledge of the Bible to rebuke the spirit in the name of Jesus.

REASON 3:

Memorizing the Word of God Guides Us to Make Right Decisions

The book of Psalms describes the Word of God as a lamp that guides us in the darkness. "Your word is a lamp to my feet and a light to my path" (Psalm 119:105, NKJV). A lamp or a light illuminates the path in the darkness, allowing a person to see where they are going. In the same way, memorizing the Word of God enlightens my life and gives me direction and clarity when I face moral, ethical, or spiritual darkness.

The principles and teachings found in the Bible serve as a foundation for helping make decisions aligned with the will of God. I remember when I found a large amount of money and was tempted to keep it because, well, I needed money. But the Word of kept ringing in my ears, and my conscience said, "Thou shalt not steal" (Exodus 20:15, KJV). I decided to take the money to the owner. Memorizing the Word of God will always guide us to make the right decision if we are in tune with the Holy Spirit.

REASON 4:

Memorizing the Word of God Prepares Us to Witness for Christ

Every disciple of Jesus has been called to be a witness for God. Testifying is not a gift; it's a result. It is the result of being with Jesus. When we treasure the Word of God in our hearts, we can be better witnesses because this results from knowing Jesus personally and intimately.

Sharing our testimony is a fruit of being connected to the Lord

Jesus Christ. And to testify more effectively, we must understand the Word of God. We must keep it in our minds and be prepared to bear witness to anyone who asks us.

The apostle Paul says, "Be wise in the way you act toward outsiders; make the most of every opportunity. Let your conversation be always full of grace, seasoned with salt, so that you may know how to answer everyone" (Colossians 4:5, 6). The wise counsel means seizing every opportunity to testify of the Savior's love. Our words must always be full of grace. But how can we speak with graceful words when our mind is full of other things? The only way to say good words is to have our hearts and minds filled with God's Word.

REASON 5:
Memorizing the Word of God Energizes and Sharpens Our Minds

There is nothing more powerful to sharpen our memory and strengthen our minds than the Word of God. Ellen G. White says, "The Bible is the only rule of faith and doctrine. And there is nothing more calculated to energize the mind, and strengthen the intellect, than the study of the Word of God. No other book is so potent to elevate the thoughts, to give vigor to the faculties, as the deep, ennobling truths of the Bible. If God's Word were studied as it should be, men would have a breadth of mind, a nobility of character, and a stability of purpose, that is rarely seen in these times."[4]

Many brain research studies show that exercising the brain helps fight Alzheimer's and dementia. We experience cognitive decline as we age, not necessarily because of the natural aging process, but because we are not using our brains as we should. The mind is just not getting enough exercise. The human mind is like a muscle that needs regular exercise, or it will become weak.

Here is what doctors are saying: "Today's research, including that of the National Institute of Aging, debunks the traditional assumption that aging and forgetfulness go together."[5] There is no evidence to prove that you cannot remember anything just because you are old. The reason for forgetfulness is not age but mental laziness. It is because we do not use our brains enough that we lose sharpness. Like the old saying, "Use it or lose it."

In his book *Ageless Memory* Harry Lorayne lists several studies proving this point. "From *The Journal of the American Medical Association*: 'More frequent participation in [mental, mind, brain] stimulating activities is associated with a reduced risk of Alzheimer's.'

"From *Modern Maturity* magazine: 'Just like the heart, the brain needs unclogged arteries to carry fresh blood and oxygen. Help your arteries stay clean by exercising. Any mental exercise . . . changes the structure of your brain. It causes the nerve cells to grow and the connections between them to strengthen.'"

Many of these studies show that using your mind to learn new things increases the number of cells in the brain and builds new neural connections, resulting in better memory. Lorayne includes a study by Dr. Marian Diamond that appeared in *Experimental Neurology*. Her research "suggests 'that nerve cells grow no matter what one's age, in response to 'intellectual enrichment' [*read use, exercise; using your imagination and memory*]—anything that stimulates the brain with novelty and change.' . . . The research concluded that 'development and growth of the brain go on into old age.'"[6]

REASON 6:

Memorizing the Word of God Allows the Holy Spirit to Remind Us of the Promises of God

The Holy Spirit inspired and led the writers of the Bible. Therefore, the only one who can help us understand the Bible is the Holy Spirit. This why Jesus told His disciples, "But the Helper, the Holy Spirit, whom the Father will send in My name, He will teach you all things, and bring to your remembrance all things that I said to you" (John 14:26, NKJV).

The Holy Spirit guides us to the truth. His role is to remind us of all the words of Jesus, convict us of sin, and to assure us of victory over sin (John 16:7-15). The Holy Spirit is called another

Comforter or Helper. Like Jesus, He reminds us of God's Word (Luke 24:25-44). "For this reason we also, since the day we heard it, do not cease to pray for you, and to ask that you may be filled with the knowledge of His will in all wisdom and spiritual understanding; that you may walk worthy of the Lord, fully pleasing Him, being fruitful in every good work and increasing in the knowledge of God" (Colossians 1:9, 10, NKJV).

We can gain spiritual understanding only by the guidance of the Holy Spirit. When we try to memorize the Word of God, the Holy Spirit actively helps us not just to memorize it but to understand it. When we memorize the Scriptures, we remember all the promises of God. Having the promises of God in our minds will be excellent protection against discouragement in the Christian life.

REASON 7:

Memorizing the Word of God Helps Us Develop the Character of Jesus

One of the goals of any disciple of Christ is to grow in the image of God. We have taken off our old self—our old ways of living—and put on the new self, which is renewed in knowledge daily in the image of God. A true disciple of Christ imitates Christ and must develop the mind of Christ.

After receiving the Holy Spirit, Christ's disciples were known to be like Christ. They thought like Christ and lived like Christ. To be a Christian is to be like Christ. In his epistle to the Philippians, the apostle Paul wrote, "In your relationships with one another, have the same mindset as Christ Jesus" (Philippians 2:5). To have the same attitude as Jesus is to have the same way of thinking as Jesus. The same mindset. To be a Christian is to be like Jesus in words, attitudes, and actions. The ideal is to have the same mind as did Jesus Christ.

If we desire to be transformed in the image of Jesus, we must look at the examples not of sinful men but of Jesus. Obviously, to think like Jesus, we need to have the Word of God in our hearts. The plan of salvation is about developing the character of Jesus.

The goal is to become fully mature disciples of Jesus.

Here is how the apostle Paul puts it: "He is the one we proclaim, admonishing, and teaching everyone with all wisdom, so that we may present everyone fully mature in Christ" (Colossians 1:28). Feeding daily on the Word of God helps us become mature disciples of Jesus.

When we pray in harmony with God's will and Word, the promise is that He will answer our prayers. "If you remain in me and my words remain in you, ask whatever you wish, and it shall be done for you" (John 15:7). Having the words of Jesus in our hearts is a key to effective prayers.

Prayer is about relationship. When we pray, trusting that God wants the best for us, He will answer our prayers—perhaps not how we want, but He will answer. And because of our close relationship with Jesus and His Word, we will know that He will in His time and in His way.

The apostle Paul, writing to the Philippians, said, "And this is my prayer: that your love may abound more and more in knowledge and depth of insight, so that you may be able to discern what is best and may be pure and blameless for the day of Christ" (Philippians 1:9, 10).

. . . LIKE JESUS

Becoming like Jesus is the ultimate goal of a disciple of Jesus. Becoming like Jesus is more than practicing religion. It is about character transformation. It is about having the mind and the character of Jesus.

Every time I ask a congregation, "How many of you want to be like Jesus?" almost everybody raises their hands. Why? Because people genuinely want to become like Jesus. But knowing how to do this can be difficult. The truth is, we can't do this ourselves— we need God to change us from the inside out. He alone transforms us when we surrender our will and way to Him. Then we ask the Holy Spirit to help us carefully and intentionally store His Word in our hearts.

Being like Christ is thinking like Christ and living like Christ.

This is why the apostle Paul says, "Let this mind be in you which was also in Christ Jesus" (Philippians 2:5, NKJV). Ellen White says, "Those who put on the whole armor of God and devote some time every day to meditation and prayer, and to the study of the Scriptures will be connected with heaven and will have a saving, transforming influence upon those around them."[7]

When we see Christ's perfect character, we naturally want to become like Him. We feel a hatred for sin, and we ask Him to shape our characters to be like His. As we learn and meditate on the Word of God, our relationship grows. As we are led by the Holy Spirit, we become participants in the divine nature. We will come to the perfection of Christ's character.

"It is one thing to treat the Bible as a book of good moral instruction, to be heeded so far as is consistent with the spirit of the times and our position in the world; it is another thing to regard it as it really is—the Word of the living God, the Word that is our life, the Word that is to mold our actions, our words, and our thoughts. To hold God's Word as anything less than this is to reject it."[8]

Here is another statement that deals with character: "The Word of God is a character-detector, a motive-tester. We are to read this Word with heart and mind open to receive the impressions that God will give. We must not think that the reading of the Word can accomplish that which only He whom the Word reveals, who stands behind the Word, can accomplish. Some are in danger of hastening to the conclusion that because they hold firmly to the doctrines of the truth, they are actually in possession of the blessings which these doctrines declare shall come to the receiver of truth. Many keep the truth in the outer court. Its sacred principles have not a controlling influence over the words, the thoughts, the actions."[9]

Storing Scripture in our minds is not merely an academic exercise but a pathway to spiritual growth. It offers a deeper understanding of God's will and equips us to face life's challenges with faith and wisdom. As we embark on this journey, we enrich our lives and become beacons of light and truth.

ACTION STEPS

1. Decide to begin memorizing the Word of God today.

2. Spend unhurried time in communion with God. Read the Bible and memorize key Bible texts that the Holy Spirit puts in your heart.

3. Trust in your memory, and the Creator who made you a wonderful creature.

4. Believe that you can learn the Bible by memory.

5. Believe that you are smarter than you think you are.

ENDNOTES

[1] Ellen G. White manuscript 67, 1898, in *Letters and Manuscripts* (Silver Spring, Md.: Ellen G. White Estate), vol. 13, p. 273.

[2] Ellen G. White, *Gospel Workers* (Washington, D.C.: Review and Herald Pub. Assn., 1915), p. 261.

[3] Ellen G. White, *Selected Messages* (Washington, D.C.: Review and Herald Pub. Assn., 1958, 1980), book 1, p. 391.

[4] Ellen G. White, in *Review and Herald*, July 17, 1888.

[5] Harry Lorayne, *Ageless Memory: The Memory Expert's Prescription for a Razor-Sharp Mind*, 1st ed. (New York: Black Dog & Leventhal, 2010), p. 13.

[6] *Ibid.*, p. 12.

[7] Ellen G. White, *Testimonies for the Church* (Mountain View, Calif.: Pacific Press Pub. Assn., 1948), vol. 5, p. 112.

[8] Ellen G. White, *Education* (Mountain View, Calif.: Pacific Press Pub. Assn., 1903), p. 260.

[9] Ellen G. White, *The Faith I Live By* (Washington, D.C.: Review and Herald Pub. Assn., 1958), p. 18.

Chapter IV

Mastering the Art of Memorizing Scripture

"If you abide in Me, and My words abide in you,
you will ask what you desire, and it shall be done for you."
—John 15:7, NKJV

I was traveling by train at night through Ukraine with a leader of the Ukrainian Union Conference of Seventh-day Adventists. Awakening at 4:00 a.m., I began my daily practice of memorizing books from the Bible. My friend asked what I was doing. I explained that I was memorizing the book of Philippians, my focus at that time.

Fascinated, he expressed a long-standing desire to memorize the Bible, but admitted his lack of know-how. I offered to teach him my simple methodology. He eagerly adopted it; a few months later he wrote, saying that he had memorized the first chapter of Philippians. "Ramón, I appreciate all the experiences we shared. They profoundly impacted me," he said. "I've mastered the first chapter of Philippians. Your model of dedication inspires and motivates me! Immense thanks!"

A SIMPLE METHOD

To start your journey toward getting to know God and learning His teachings, you must have an intense longing to commit

God's Word to memory. Nothing significant can be achieved in life without a deep-seated desire to make it happen. There's a comprehensive technique for embedding the Word of God in your mind. Although there are many suggestions for Bible memorization, here's a simple approach to begin with.

A. Have a Burning Desire

The journey to memorize Scripture begins with a genuine craving to know God and internalize His Word. You likely already have this desire, since you're reading this book, but if you don't, I encourage you to pray about it. Ask God to place this desire in your heart or in the heart of your spouse or children so that you can begin to memorize the Bible together. Initially your desire may be feeble, but you can ask God to fortify and intensify it through prayer.

B. Pray

The second step is to ask God for help. Claim Mathew 7:7, 8, which says, "Ask and it will be given to you; seek and you will find; knock and the door will be opened to you. For everyone who asks receives; the one who seeks finds; and to the one who knocks, the door will be opened."

So you pray: "Dear God, You said in Your Word, 'Ask, and it will be given to you.' I am asking You right now to answer this prayer. I want to memorize this Bible passage. Would You please help me to put it in my heart? Please send Your Holy Spirit to remind me of the words I learn. I will do my part by reading it, reviewing it, analyzing it, and meditating on it. But I need the Holy Spirit to help me remember it. Thank You, Father."

C. Act by Faith

Move forward in faith, trusting that God will help you memorize His living Word. Here's how you can do it: First, choose the Bible version that you love the most or the one you feel the Holy Spirit is impressing you to place in your heart. Once you have picked a Bible version, stick with that version.

After selecting your Bible version, choose a book from the Bible. (Don't worry; you will learn one verse at a time before memorizing the whole book.) After you have chosen your book, pray again and ask God to help you memorize it. Then you can start with the book's first chapter.

Once you have selected your book and the first chapter to memorize, count the number of verses in each chapter. For example, if you begin with Philippians, you will notice that it has four chapters and that the first chapter has 30 verses. This will give you an overview of the book and will help you organize the process in your mind.

Before you begin to memorize the first line, you need to prepare yourself. Here are some of the things you will need:

☑ **Your favorite Bible**

☑ **A notebook or loose sheets of paper**

☑ **A quality pen or pencil that you enjoy writing with**

Once you have gathered these items, find a quiet place. Now you are ready to begin

1. Choose the chapter you want to memorize.

2. Pray for the Holy Spirit to help you memorize the chapter.

3. Read it several times.

4. Break it down into logical sections.

   Example: To memorize Luke 11:13, NKJV:

   a. "**If you then, being evil,**

   b. know how to give **good gifts** to your children,

   c. **how much more** will your heavenly Father

   d. give the Holy Spirit to **those who ask Him!**"

5. Record the text with your own voice and listen to it as many times as possible.

6. Use your imagination. Think about the meaning. Think about the story or the imagery in the text. See it in your mind.

7. Write it down from memory.

Repeat out loud each section multiple times. Then pray the text. For example, you might pray, "Lord, I'm evil, yet I know how to give good gifts to my children. How much more will You, my heavenly Father, give the Holy Spirit to me when I ask You!" Learn it; obey it; teach it to someone else; and repeat the process.

Read the first sentence of the verse out loud. Usually the verse has natural sentences, but sometimes you may have to break the text in a way that makes more sense to you. For example, if you want to memorize Philippians 2:1, NIV, here's how you can break down the verse:

Verse 1:

a. "Therefore, if you have any **encouragement** from _being united with Christ_,

b. if any **comfort** from his love,

c. if any **common sharing** in the Spirit,

d. if any **tenderness and compassion**,"

You will notice how easy it is to learn the verse once you break it down into natural sentences, or key words or ideas. Also, notice that I highlighted the key words or phrases in each sentence. Those are the key words to remember.

Once you have done that, you will read the whole verse one sentence at a time as you write them on a piece of paper or in your notebook. I recommend loose sheets of paper that you can throw away once you finish memorizing each section.

Repeat each sentence at least seven times. You write the verse, you think about its meaning, you read it out loud, and then you meditate on God's message for you.

Once you learn each sentence individually, it is time to connect them. You do this by reading it out loud 21 times in groups of seven. You repeat it seven times, stop for a minute and repeat it, then stop for a minute or so and repeat it again, for a total of 21. The more you repeat the text, the easier it becomes for your mind to store the information long-term. This is how the mind transfers crucial information from short-term to long-term memory.

FORMING A HABIT

You have numerous habits—actions that you perform automatically, without even thinking about them. This is how the brain functions. When your brain identifies a piece of information that you will use regularly, it stores that information. Therefore, the more we vocalize the verses, the easier it will be for the mind to solidify them as part of our daily routine.

Habits are things that you do consistently and automatically. You don't even need to think about it. That is why the more you recite the verses aloud, the easier it will become for your mind to fix it as part of a daily routine. Imagine the excitement of having the Word of God flowing out of you. Think of the blessing this will be for you, your family, those around you, your prayer life, and the proclamation of the gospel to others.

There is compelling scientific evidence that shows that using our minds to memorize and learn new things, even at mature ages, helps deter dementia and Alzheimer's disease. So that is a bonus to the tremendous experience of writing the Word of God in our hearts.

MEDITATING ON GOD'S WORD

Meditate on the text throughout the day. As you read the text, think about it. Pray about it. God gives us spiritual "bread" when we read, and He lovingly speaks truth into our lives exactly when we need it. Consider the special meaning of the text you're memorizing and its personal meaning in your life. Psalm 1 says that those who meditate in the Word of God "day and night" will prosper. Memorizing Scripture can be integrated into your daily routine by repeating the verses out loud during various activities.

Here are some suggestions:

1. When you wake up in the morning, embrace the day, filling your morning with the Word.

2. When you have trouble falling asleep, instead of tossing and turning in bed, invite tranquility into your sleepless nights by reciting Bible verses.

3. When you're stuck in traffic, turn the tedious moments into meaningful ones by listening to recorded Bible texts.

4. When you travel, enhance your experiences and journeys by memorizing Scripture.

5. Transform your shower or bath into a peaceful sanctuary for repeating Bible verses.

6. When waiting on the phone, transcend the tediousness by thinking of Bible verses.

7. Make the verses you are learning part of your morning or evening devotion. Integrate recitation into your morning or evening devotion, making it an essential part of your spiritual growth.

Enjoy the process and take pleasure in the progress.

> *"You will show me the path of life;*
> *In Your presence is fullness of joy;*
> *At Your right hand are pleasures forevermore."*
> —Psalm 16:11, NKJV

At this point you have likely woven several powerful, life-transforming Bible verses into the fabric of your heart. To solidify their presence in your memory, recite them with fervor and passion, allowing them to become a part of you.

ACTION STEPS

Practice! Here are four Bible texts you can memorize this week.

Day 1: Luke 11:13, NKJV

1. **"If you then, being evil,**

2. know how to give *good gifts* to your children,

3. **how much more** will your heavenly Father give the Holy Spirit *to those who ask Him!"*

Day 2: Acts 1:8, NKJV

1. But you shall receive **power**

2. when the *Holy Spirit* has come upon you;

3. and you shall be **witnesses to Me**

4. in *Jerusalem*, and in all *Judea* and *Samaria*, and to the **end of the earth.**

Day 3: 2 Corinthians 3:18, NKJV

1. <u>**But we all**</u>, with unveiled face,

2. beholding **as in a mirror** the glory of the Lord,

3. are being *transformed* into the same image from glory to glory,

4. just as by the **Spirit of the Lord.**

Day 4: Galatians 2:20, NKJV

1. *I have been crucified with Christ*;

2. it is **no longer I who live**, but Christ lives in me;

3. and the **life which I now live in the flesh** I live by faith in the Son of God,

4. *who loved me and gave Himself for me.*

Even though the Bible doesn't specifically refer to the modern practice of memorizing Scripture, it stresses the significance of keeping God's Word in our hearts, reflecting on it constantly, and implementing it in our daily lives. All these aspects affirm the importance of memorizing God's Word. Rather than just an activity, it should be integrated into our daily lives as a way of living. Memorizing the Word of God should not be something we simply do as disciples of Christ; instead, it should be a part of who we are.

ACTION STEPS

Seven Bible Verses You Can Memorize Today

Each of the following verses offers a unique perspective as to why you should hide God's Word in your heart. Begin storing them in your mind today.

Day 1: Psalm 119:11, NKJV

"Your word I have **hidden in my heart**,

that I might not sin against You."

Day 2: Joshua 1:8, NKJV

"This Book of the Law shall not depart from your mouth,

but you shall **meditate in it day and night**,

that you may observe to do according to all that is written

in it.

For then you will make your way prosperous,

and then you will have good success."

Day 3: Colossians 3:16, NKJV

"Let the word of Christ **dwell in you richly** in all

wisdom,

teaching and admonishing one another in psalms and

hymns and spiritual songs,

singing with grace in your hearts to the Lord."

Day 4: Hebrews 4:12, NKJV

"For the word of God *is* **living and powerful**,

and sharper than any two-edged sword,

piercing even to the division of soul and spirit,

and of joints and marrow, and is a discerner of the

thoughts and intents of the heart."

Day 5: James 1:21, NKJV

"Therefore lay aside all filthiness and overflow of

wickedness,

and receive with meekness the **implanted word**,

which is able to save your souls."

Day 6: Psalm 1:2, NKJV

"But **his delight** is in the law of the Lord,

and in His law he **meditates day and night**."

Day 7: 2 Timothy 3:16, 17, ESV

"All Scripture is breathed out by God and **profitable for**

teaching,

for reproof, for correction, and for training in

righteousness,

that the man of God may be competent,

equipped for every good work."

Each verse highlights the transformative power of God's Word when hidden in the heart. As you memorize them, meditate on their meaning and how they apply to your daily life.

Chapter V
Seven Daily Activities That Can Make You Smarter

*"Let the word of Christ dwell in you richly in all wisdom,
teaching and admonishing one another in psalms and hymns
and spiritual songs, singing with grace in your hearts to the Lord."*
—Colossians 3:16, NKJV

*"The minds of all who make the Word of God their study
will enlarge."*
—Ellen G. White manuscript 67, 1898, in *Letters and Manuscripts*, vol. 13, p. 273

Bertha was a rich woman who spent most of her time in casinos. Every week she would gamble, spending not just her time and her money but also her life. She did this for many years in order to combat loneliness and sadness after the tragic death of her husband, who had been a high-ranking U.S. marine. However, despite her time in the casinos, she was not happy. Nothing brought her joy and peace. She was depressed and hopeless when we met her.

My friend and I were visiting the neighborhood when we knocked on her door. She was wearing skimpy clothes when she invited us in. My friend and I looked at each other and felt a little uncomfortable about entering the house. But we quickly shared the reason for our visit, wanting to leave as soon as possible because we thought that we had interrupted her. But she insisted, "Come in, please!" Hesitantly we went in, not knowing what to expect. She asked us to sit down. We did, and began sharing the Word of God.

After a few minutes we noticed a tear coming down her cheek, and she excused herself. She came back from her bedroom dressed more appropriately. We felt more comfortable and continued sharing. Then Bertha said, "You know, I don't know the Bible. I don't know God. I don't know how to pray. But I have been asking, 'God, if You exist, please send me someone to teach me the Bible.' Here is some money. Please buy a Bible for me."

We bought the Bible and continued to study with her. After a while she and her entire family were baptized. She later told us that she used to spend thousands of dollars gambling in the casino, looking for peace of mind. But now she knows that the only one who brings peace, joy, and happiness is Jesus.

Bertha chose learning the Bible over casinos, and her life was never the same. It reminds me of Jesus' words, in John 7:37: "On the last day, that great day of the feast, Jesus stood and cried out, saying, 'If anyone thirst, let him come to Me and drink'" (NKJV).

Jesus came to offer us the best possible life on earth now, and eternal life on the new earth. This is our destiny and our hope. God created us to live abundantly. By studying, learning, obeying, and meditating on the Word of God, we can experience this amazing life. However, wisdom comes only from God.

"If any of you lacks wisdom, let him ask of God, who gives to all liberally and without reproach, and it will be given to him" (James 1:5, NKJV). Therefore, the first thing we must do to get more wisdom is to ask God for spiritual wisdom through the Holy Spirit. Only wise people can live the abundant life that Jesus offers.

Here are seven activities that can help you enjoy this powerful life and become wiser as you seek to grow in your walk with Jesus.

1. HANDWRITING THE BIBLE

Writing by hand can improve mental activity. Many studies suggest that handwriting produces deeper electrical activity in the brain. Consequently, handwriting forces the brain to learn more and to retain what has been learned. This is why educational institutions are trying to adopt policies that ensure children receive minimum training in cursive writing.

Audrey van der Meer, a neuroscientist and professor at the

Norwegian University of Science and Technology, discovered, "The use of pen and paper gives the brain more 'hooks' to hang your memories on. Writing by hand creates much more activity in the sensorimotor parts of the brain. A lot of senses are activated by pressing the pen on paper, seeing the letters you write, and hearing the sound you make while writing. These sense experiences create contact between different parts of the brain and open the brain up for learning. We both learn better and remember better."[1]

Dr. William R. Klemm, in his article "Why Writing by Hand Could Make You Smarter," says that researchers have found surprising evidence for setting the keyboard aside and grabbing pen and paper. "In the case of learning cursive writing, the brain develops 'functional specialization' that integrates both sensation, movement control, and thinking," Klemm says. "Brain imaging studies reveal that multiple areas of the brain become co-activated during the learning of cursive writing of pseudo-letters, as opposed to typing or just visual practice."[2]

Data from van der Meer's research shows that "cursive handwriting primed the brain for learning by synchronizing brain waves in the theta rhythm range (4-7 Hz). . . . Such oscillatory neuronal activity in these particular brain areas is important for memory and for the encoding of new information and, therefore, provides the brain with optimal conditions for learning,"[3]

Here is the conclusion of these studies: "We conclude that because of the benefits of sensory-motor integration due to the larger involvement of the senses as well as fine and precisely controlled hand movements when writing by hand and when drawing, it is vital to maintain both activities in a learning environment to facilitate and optimize learning."[4]

Technology has rendered handwriting unnecessary, to where many people consider writing by hand useless. However, handwriting can enhance our cognitive functions. Engaging as many senses as possible in our efforts to write the Word of God in our hearts will result in better retention and a superior ability to recall the Bible verses stored in the mind.

ACTION STEPS

1. Handwrite the Bible verses you want to commit to memory daily.

2. Use the *Inverse Young Adult Sabbath School Bible Study Guide* for a daily experience in handwriting the Word of God.

3. Write a sentence or two asking God for spiritual wisdom in order to memorize His Word.

4. As you write the Bible verse, ask the Holy Spirit to help you fix it in your mind.

2. GETTING EXERCISE

Walking is the single most important exercise we can do. Even though God does not need exercise, the Bible talks about God walking in the cool of the day (Genesis 3:8). Walking while listening to the Bible early in the morning will help you memorize it. Exercise is the fountain of youth. When coupled with prayer and listening to the Bible, it is a powerful habit to boost energy and enhance quality of life.

We were not created to sit for hours in front of the TV, the computer, or committees. We were designed to work in the garden. We were made for outdoor movement, just like everything in the universe. There are many types of exercise, but walking is popular and easy. Briskly walking daily for 30 minutes can help you stay healthy and will do wonders for your brain.

My wife and I enjoy walking early in the morning for 60 minutes. That daily walk is a powerful stress reducer and helps us face any challenges during the day.

God desires to bless us as He blessed Enoch when he walked with Him. When we meditate on the Word of God while walking, our brains receive physical, mental, and spiritual exercise. Adam and Eve walked and talked with God face-to-face before the Fall. Enoch, Noah, Abraham, Paul, and many other followers of Christ walked with God by faith. When Jesus healed the man at the Pool of Bethesda, He commanded him, "Get up! Pick up your mat and walk" (John 5:8). Jesus wasn't giving the paralytic man a command to exercise, but I often wonder, what if we were to follow that simple command? "Get up and walk." How much would our health improve?

Walking can help you burn more calories, lower your blood pressure, improve your heart health, reduce the risk of diabetes, and energize your brain. Anything that improves brain activity sharpens our minds and enhances our ability to remember what we learn.

When we exercise, fresh oxygenated blood rushes into the brain, thus improving memory. Dr. Holly Schiff says, "Walking sends increased blood flow to the brain, which is linked to better cognitive function, protection against decline and improved memory." Exercise also enlarges the hippocampus, where long-term memory resides. Schiff says, "Walking reduces stress, anxiety, and fatigue, and reduces your risk of becoming depressed—so it is also beneficial for your mental health."[5]

William Mayle, in his article "Incredible Things That Happen When You Walk More, Say Experts," reports, "According to a study published in the *British Journal of Sports Medicine*, the daily act of performing 30 minutes of moderate-intensity exercise—such as brisk walking—not only improves your cognitive performance, but it also improves the cognitive functions associated with smarter and better decisions. Win win!"[6]

Science links exercise with improving brain capacity. We need to spend more time walking rather than sitting. Do it for your body, and do it for your mind.

ACTION STEPS

1. Schedule exercise daily.
2. Walk briskly for 30-60 minutes daily.
3. Stretch your body before and after your walk to avoid injuries.
4. Meditate on a Bible text you want to commit to memory. Repeat it in your mind.

3. MEMORIZING THE WORD OF GOD

Research shows that any brain exercise will improve memory and reduce the possibility of dementia and Alzheimer's. However, nothing is more powerful to keep your brain young than to fill it with the God's Word.

Ellen G. White puts it this way: "The Bible is the best book in the world for giving intellectual culture. Its study taxes the mind, strengthens the memory, and sharpens the intellect more than the study of all the subjects that human philosophy embraces. The great themes which it presents, the dignified simplicity with which these themes are handled, the light which is shed upon the great problems of life, bring strength and vigor to the understanding."[7]

ACTION STEPS

1. Commit five Bible verses to memory every single day.
2. Begin with one verse a day and add more as you feel confident in the Lord.
3. Ask the Holy Spirit to help you remember what you have learned.
4. Review your Bible texts daily.

4. DRINKING PLENTY OF WATER

You have probably heard the counsel that you should drink eight glasses of water every day. That seems to be the simple, scientific rule for drinking water. But who's counting?

I always thought that I was fully hydrated because I daily drank two or three glasses of water plus juices or tea. Then I started to get muscle cramps and headaches. All these symptoms stopped when I began to drink a lot of water. Now I begin my day drinking 20 to 40 ounces of water in the morning before breakfast. I drink another 20 to 30 ounces during the day. That works great for me. (But everyone is different.)

The human body is more than 60 percent water, the brain about 90 percent. These facts show the importance of drinking plenty of water. Dehydration can impair your efforts to memorize the Bible—or anything else, for that matter. Losing as little as 3 percent of your body's water content can harm your ability to memorize.

It is recommended that you drink at least 1.9 liters, or about 64 ounces, of water daily. The more water you drink, the better for your brain. If you want to improve your memory so you can memorize Scripture, drink more pure water.

ACTION STEPS

1. Drink 64 ounces of water every day.
2. If possible, have a pitcher of water with a few pieces of lemon in your kitchen at room temperature.
3. Drink as much water as possible early in the morning.
4. Reduce water intake after 6:00 p.m. to avoid trips to the bathroom at night.

5. EATING A SIMPLE PLANT-BASED DIET

In 1826 the French lawyer and famous gastronome Jean-Anthelme Brillant-Savarin wrote in the book *The Physiology of Taste* this well-known statement: "Tell me what you eat and I will tell you what you are."[8] He implied that what a person is mentally, physically, and emotionally is determined by what they put in their mouth. Today we can take issue with this argument, but the fact remains: food can help or hinder our ability to think, reason, and memorize.

"Eat right, exercise, die anyway," the saying goes, and correctly, too. Even if we have the best diet and exercise regularly, we still die. Even eating bread from heaven, manna, didn't keep the Israelites in the wilderness from dying. The point? Despite eating the best food in the world, they still passed away.

"While they were eating, Jesus took bread, and when he had given thanks, he broke it and gave it to his disciples, saying, 'Take and eat; this is my body'" (Matthew 26:26). When you memorize the Word of God daily, you are, as it were, eating the body of Jesus.

The words of God are to be eaten daily for spiritual life in order to make the soul flourish.

ACTION STEPS

1. Choose to avoid consuming anything that may hurt your brain.
2. Commit to a simple, well-balanced, plant-based diet. Incorporate brain-boosting foods such as leafy greens, cruciferous vegetables, nuts, and blueberries into your meals.
3. Avoid overeating; it can hurt your cognitive abilities.

6. GETTING ENOUGH SLEEP

Getting a good night's sleep is crucial for our well-being. It helps restore our body and mind, allowing us to function the best. Experts recommend sleeping seven to eight hours nightly. It can significantly contribute to a sharper mind and better memory retention. On the other hand, lack of sleep can harm the brain, leading to impaired cognitive abilities and memory loss. Therefore, prioritizing sleep is essential for maintaining good health and for memorizing the Bible.

I have the habit of writing the Bible verses and chapters I am memorizing as soon as I get up. And I have noticed something amazing. When I have a good night's sleep, which in my case means seven to eight hours, my handwriting is neat, clear, and legible. But when I don't get a good night's sleep, I tend to scribble, and my handwriting looks terrible. To me, that says something about sleep and brain function.

ACTION STEPS

1. Establishing a consistent bedtime routine is recommended. Try to go to bed at the same time every night.
2. Getting enough sleep is crucial for maintaining good health. Aim to get seven to eight hours of sleep.

3. Spend the first 10 minutes after you go to bed reciting one chapter of the Bible that you want to commit to memory.

7. EXERCISING SELF-DISCIPLINE

Self-discipline is the ability to do what you know you should do, whether you like it or not. Self-discipline is about saying no to the things that harm us and yes to the things that are good for us. It is about self-control.

Another word for self-control is temperance. Temperance is the ability to enjoy the good things in life while rejecting the harmful. In a practical way, we need self-control to say no to such substances as drugs, alcohol, tobacco, and caffeine. All these have been linked to reduced cognitive performance.

When you look at the Bible record for an example of self-control, Daniel comes to mind. Once offered food contrary to his simple, healthful diet, he refused. When he and his friends opted for a simpler plant-based diet and water, they became 10 times smarter than the rest of the wise men of Babylon (Daniel 1).

It should be noted that although these practices can support a healthy brain, individual results may vary. It's always best to talk with your health-care provider before making big changes to your diet, exercise, or lifestyle. Also, some cultures (extremely cold countries) have little access to fresh food or even legumes.

ACTION STEPS

1. Practice self-control by saying no to harmful drugs, alcohol, tobacco, coffee, and caffeinated energy drinks.
2. Ask the Holy Spirit to give you self-discipline every day.
3. Practice activities that help improve your mental capacities.

———————————

ENDNOTES

[1]Norwegian University of Science and Technology, "Why Writing by Hand Makes Kids Smarter," *ScienceDaily*, Oct. 1, 2020, www.sciencedaily.com/releases /2020/10/201001113540.htm.

[2] William Klemm, "Why Writing by Hand Could Make You Smarter," *Psychology Today*, March 14, 2013, https://www.psychologytoday.com/us/blog/memory-medic/201303/why-writing-hand-could-make-you-smarter.

[3] Christopher Bergland, "Why Cursive Handwriting Is Good for Your Brain," *Psychology Today*, Oct. 2, 2020, https://www.psychologytoday.com/us/blog/the-athletes-way/202010/why-cursive-handwriting-is-good-for-your-brain.

[4] Eva Ose Askvik, F. R. (Ruud) van der Weel, Audrey L. H. van der Meer, "The Importance of Cursive Handwriting Over Typewriting for Learning in the Classroom: A High-Density EEG Study of 12-Year-Old Children and Young Adults," *Frontiers in Psychology* 11 (July 28, 2020): 1810, https://www.ncbi.nlm.nih.gov/pmc/articles/PMC7399101/.

[5] In William Mayle, "Incredible Things That Happen When You Walk More, Say Experts," *Eat This, Not That*, June 15, 2021, https://www.eatthis.com/incredible-things-that-happen-when-you-walk-more-say-experts/.

[6] *Ibid.*

[7] Ellen G. White, *Gospel Workers* (Washington, D.C.: Review and Herald Pub. Assn., 1915), p. 100.

[8] Jean Anthelme Brillat-Savarin, *The Physiology of Taste* (Paris: Chez A. Sautelet et Cie, 1826).

Chapter VI
A Call Back to the Fundamentals

"But his delight is in the law of the Lord,
And in His law he meditates day and night.
He shall be like a tree
Planted by the rivers of water,
That brings forth its fruit in its season,
Whose leaf also shall not wither;
And whatever he does shall prosper."
—Psalm 1:2, 3, NKJV

In July 1961 Vince Lombardi, the celebrated head coach of the Green Bay Packers, established what would later become a legendary chapter in American football history. His approach to the first day of training camp was unconventional, particularly after what had occurred during the previous season. The Packers had suffered a morale-crushing defeat to the Philadelphia Eagles, squandering a lead in the fourth quarter of the NFL Championship game.

The football players eagerly awaited the new season's training camp. They were a skilled and experienced team, confident in their abilities and looking forward to building on the previous season's success. They were ready to explore new strategies and innovative plays. However, Lombardi had a different plan in mind.

The moment that Lombardi held up a football during their first meeting and stated, "Gentlemen, this is a football!" has become iconic. This moment was not merely a statement but a philosophy. The philosophy was to go back to basics and focus on of the game, the core elements of football excellence: blocking, tackling, throwing, and catching.

Despite misgiving by some of the players, Lombardi's philosophy proved effective. By starting from scratch and focusing on the game's fundamentals, the team strengthened their skills and improved their overall performance, leading to great success. Lombardi's philosophy of focusing on the fundamentals is still considered a valuable lesson that coaches and players follow today.

This emphasis on mastering the basics paid off spectacularly. The Packers' season culminated in a dominant victory: the team won the NFL Championship with a staggering 37–0 triumph over the New York Giants, and then went on to five NFL Championships in seven years.

The Lombardi approach underscores a powerful lesson that extends far beyond sports. In the church we always seek new resources and methods to reach people with the gospel of Jesus Christ. But we often overlook the importance of fundamental principles. Prayer, Bible study, and meditation on the Word of God are the fundamentals of discipleship. Focusing on these core elements can lead to extraordinary achievements in leadership, discipleship, evangelism, and church planting. Applying the same principle in our personal and professional lives can lead to exceptional results. The lesson is clear: enduring success is found in a steadfast commitment to the fundamentals, not by chasing after the next big thing.

COMMUNING WITH GOD

Back to the Bible is a call to return to the central principles that made Christianity a powerful religion. It urges us to focus on what truly matters: our relationship with God through prayer and reflection on His Word. Over the years several spiritual disciplines, such as prayer, meditation, and the study of the Scriptures, have been acknowledged as essential for the existence of a rich spiritual life.

Prayer is essential. A life without prayer is not a spiritual life, because it is through prayer that we connect with the Holy Spirit. Nobody will deny that Jesus was a spiritual man. He was a godly man. He was in tune with the Holy Spirit from the day He was born until the day He died.

"Very early in the morning, while it was still dark, Jesus got up, left the house and went off to a solitary place, where he prayed" (Mark 1:35). Some biblical passages indicate that Jesus not only got up early to pray but also spent whole nights praying (Luke 6:12). And He also prayed earnestly (Luke 22:44).

Jesus is the perfect example of one who prays. He realized that He needed to be in constant connection with the Father for Him to be able to accomplish His mission. The 11 disciples of Jesus followed His example. They prayed for 10 days between Jesus' ascension and the receiving of the Holy Spirit (Acts 1:14).

E. M. Bounds says, "The key of all missionary success is prayer."[1] Every study of growing, dynamic churches reveals that prayer has a central place in their ministry. No church can begin to accomplish what God is calling them to do without prayer. It is simple. We cannot do God's work without God.

Church members are ill-equipped if we fill our heads with knowledge and methodology but fail to pray. Prayer is to the spirit what air is to the body. The Bible says that the body without the spirit is dead (James 2:26), and so are we if we fail to pray. Without prayer, the Christian is dead. Consequently, to succeed in our walk with God, prayer must be practiced, not just taught and learned.

PRIORITIZING PRAYER

When prayer becomes a priority, it reflects our deep commitment to God. Prayer is a way to connect with God, to seek His guidance, and to express gratitude. It is a way to find strength and comfort in times of difficulty and to grow in faith and spiritual understanding.

Jesus emphasized the importance of seeking God's kingdom and righteousness above all else. "Seek ye first the kingdom of God, and his righteousness; and all these things shall be added unto you" (Matthew 6:33, KJV). This means that when we prioritize God in our lives, everything else falls into place. We do not need to worry about our material needs or desires, as God will provide for us according to His will.

Prayer is not just a religious ritual; it is a way of life. It is a continuous conversation with God and how we stay connected with Him throughout the day. By prioritizing prayer, we invite God into every aspect of our lives, and we open ourselves up to His guidance and blessings.

When we make prayer a priority, we make God a priority. We demonstrate our commitment to Him, and we open ourselves up to His love and grace. As we seek God's kingdom and righteousness, we can trust that He will provide for our needs and guide us on the path of life.

To pray means to depend on God. When I pray, it means that I recognize my weaknesses and that I am powerless without Christ. Preaching the gospel to the whole world is a very sacred commission; it is a spiritual commission, and only spiritual people should endeavor to do it. That is why when Jesus sent His disciples to go make disciples, He promised them that He was going to be with them always, even to the end (Matthew 28:20).

Jesus taught them that dependence on Him was crucial., "Without Me you can do nothing" (John 15:5, NKJV). Paul echoed that thought in his letter to the Philippians when he wrote, "I can do all things in Christ who strengthens me" (Philippians 4:13, NKJV).

We become fruitful and productive servants of the Lord when we abide in Jesus. We grow and multiply when we are connected to the Vine. That connection is made possible through a consistent life of prayer.

Prayer is not just something we do; it is something we embody. Prayer was very natural for Jesus. He did not have to drag Himself out of bed to pray. For Him, prayer was not a dreadful exercise. He loved to pray. Prayer for Him was pleasant communication with His Father.

Prayer is unnatural for us because we are not used to praying. It is unnatural to us because we are more connected with sin than with God. Therefore, we tend to reject the heavenly atmosphere that prayer brings. However, we can teach ourselves to be like Jesus. We can teach ourselves to enjoy prayer and long for the precious moments of communion with God.

Ellen G. White comments, "As we make Christ our daily companion we shall feel that the powers of an unseen world are all around us; and by looking unto Jesus we shall become assimilated to His image. By beholding we become changed. The character is softened, refined, and ennobled for the heavenly kingdom. The sure result of our intercourse and fellowship with our Lord will be to increase piety, purity, and fervor. There will be a growing intelligence in prayer. We are receiving a divine education, and this is illustrated in a life of diligence and zeal."[2]

Because prayer is so important in the life of the Christian, Ellen White emphasizes that it must be our first business. "We should flee to the Word of God and to prayer, individually seeking the Lord earnestly, that we may find Him. We should make this our first business."[3]

She also points out that prayer must be accompanied by a spirit of gratitude and praise, and that prayer is not something we do occasionally; it must be constant. "Pray, pray earnestly and without ceasing, but do not forget to praise. It becomes every child of God to vindicate His character. You can magnify the Lord; you can show the power of sustaining grace. There are multitudes who do not appreciate the great love of God nor the divine compassion of Jesus."[4]

The text emphasizes the importance of spending time in solitary prayer for any disciple of Jesus. Through private, personal prayer we can receive the wisdom and power that we need in order to fulfill the work the Lord has called us to. This prayer aims to establish a deep and meaningful connection with the Almighty, just as Jesus did.

By spending time in solitary prayer and focusing on the life of Jesus, disciples can quiet their minds and focus on their spiritual growth. This allows them to reflect on their faith and draw closer to God. The practice of prayer helps create a sense of peace and calm, which is essential for hearing God's voice and receiving His guidance.

Jesus prayed for hours, often withdrawing to a solitary place. His devotion to prayer allowed Him to gain strength and discernment from the Father, which He used to minister to others. His example serves as an inspiration for all Christians to follow.

Spending time in solitary prayer reflecting on the Word of God is vital. It is how we can receive the wisdom and power that we need to fulfill God's calling. It allows us to connect to the Almighty in a deep and meaningful way, as Jesus did.

Ellen White advised, "It was in hours of solitary prayer that Jesus in his earthly life received wisdom and power. Let the youth follow his example in finding at dawn and twilight a quiet season for communion with their Father in heaven. And throughout the day let them lift up their hearts to God."[5]

I had been praying a long time for my sister to accept Jesus as her Lord and Savior. During my visits I would bring her books, Bibles, audio sermons, magazines, anything that I thought could help her understand the gospel. For 30 years I tried through my prayers to plant the seed of the gospel in her heart.

Finally I heard that a famous evangelist was going to hold meetings near her house in New York City. Intending to invite her to the meetings, I decided to visit her. I am glad that I never gave up on her; unfortunately, she refused to attend the meetings despite my efforts. So I went alone.

While attending the church service, I saw someone who resembled my sister walking toward the front of the church in response to the speaker's altar call. At first I thought it couldn't be her since she didn't know how to get to that church. But when she turned around, I was surprised to see my sister there, giving her life to Jesus Christ.

I asked her what happened, as she had other things to do, which was her excuse to me why she could not come. She replied that while she was taking a shower, a small voice told her to attend the meetings. So she asked her daughter to find the address, and took a taxi.

She said, "It felt like an irresistible force was pulling me toward the meetings, and I didn't understand it." I told her that I had been praying without ceasing for this moment for more than 30 years.

BREATHE PRAYER

The Bible contains an often overlooked but crucial command for our spiritual lives. "Pray without ceasing" (1 Thessalonians 5:17, KJV). In other words, do not stop praying.

Just as the body cannot survive without breathing, the soul cannot survive without prayer. That is why we are commanded to never stop praying. But what does that mean? How can we pray without ceasing? Is that even practical? I must confess that there was a time I had a hard time praying for more than 10 minutes, let alone all day.

"Praying without ceasing" is about praying a lot all day. Overwhelmed by the heavy responsibilities of our new position, my wife, Aurora, and I asked a friend how we could deal with this. I will never forget her response. "Pray," she said, "like crazy."

Aurora and I took that counsel seriously. We are living in a time that we must pray like crazy and at all times. Memorizing the Word of God helps us pray without ceasing as we meditate on it and on the life of Jesus. It is about maintaining a constant attitude of prayer and a deep, ongoing daily awareness of God's presence.

It doesn't necessarily imply nonstop, active prayer, as that would be impractical. Instead, it is about keeping our thoughts attuned to spiritual matters, being mindful of God's presence in every situation, and being open to spiritual insights.

Praying without ceasing is about restoring the family altar. We have an established worship routine throughout the day, such as family worship in the morning and evening. We have set aside specific times for quiet reflection and communication with God. Praying without ceasing is also about turning everyday tasks and decisions into opportunities for prayer: offering thanks, seeking guidance, or praying for others.

As I write, I know friends are praying for me and how the book will turn out. Praying without ceasing is about cultivating a continual sense of gratitude and thankfulness toward God. We can use any special moment as a prompt to pray, such as when you're worried, thankful, joyful, or faced with a decision.

Praying without ceasing means spending unrushed time meditating on the life of Jesus and in the Word. It means focusing our hearts and minds on the spiritual truth that the Holy Spirit is teaching you then. Prayer becomes a natural and integral part of our lives, almost like breathing. It becomes a continuous background activity of the heart and mind.

This approach emphasizes an ongoing, intimate relationship

with God rather than relegating prayer to specific times or rituals. Ellen G. White wrote, "Several times each day precious, golden moments should be consecrated to prayer and the study of the Scriptures, if it is only to commit a text to memory, that spiritual life may exist in the soul."[6]

In the book of Colossians the apostle Paul wrote that he prayed without ceasing for the Colossians. "For this reason we also, since the day we heard it, do not cease to pray for you, and to ask that you may be filled with the knowledge of His will in all wisdom and spiritual understanding" (Colossians 1:9, NKJV).

MEDITATING ON JESUS AND HIS WORD

Meditation is the response of a grateful heart to a gracious God. Like prayer, meditation is a spiritual discipline lost in Christianity. We live in a very busy world and a hectic society. Sometimes we are preoccupied with getting things done so that the most important thing—establishing and maintaining a closer relationship with Jesus—remains undone.

Some people in Christianity reject meditation because they associate it with Eastern religions, such as Buddhism, Hinduism, and Taoism. The goal in Eastern meditation is typically described as reaching a state of emptiness, silence, or oneness with the universe. In contrast, biblical meditation emphasizes filling the mind rather than emptying it. This type of meditation involves deep, reflective thought on the words of God in the Bible.

Bible memorization plays a crucial role in biblical meditation. By memorizing Scripture, we have a reservoir of divine wisdom to draw upon for meditation, to help us grow as disciples of Jesus. This memorization is not just about retaining words but about embedding the essence and teachings of God's Word in our hearts and minds. It serves as a foundation for meditation, enabling us to reflect deeply on these truths, understand them more profoundly, and apply them always.

In the book of Psalms the difference between the righteous and the wicked is that the righteous meditate on God, His words, and His works. The wicked meditate on their wickedness. Bible memorization gives the energy to meditation. Many psalms encourage meditation:

➢ On the law of the Lord: "But his delight is in the law of the Lord, and in his law he meditates day and night" (Psalm 1:2, NKJV).

➢ On God: "When I remember thee upon my bed, and meditate on thee in the night watches" (Psalm 63:6, KJV).

➢ On God's work: "I will meditate on all thy work, and muse on thy mighty deeds" (Psalm 77:12, RSV).

➢ On God's Word: "I have more understanding than all my teachers; for thy testimonies are my meditation" (Psalm 119:99, KJV).

Meditation must be pure and spiritual to be pleasing to God: "May my meditation be pleasing to him" (Psalm 104:34). Ellen G. White said that much meditation is needed for the success of the work. "There should be much prayer, much meditation, for this is highly necessary for the success and prosperity of the work. A spirit of traffic should not be allowed in anyone who is connected with the office. If it is permitted, the work will be neglected and marred. Common things will be placed too much upon a level with sacred things."[7]

She also says that Satan knows how important prayer and meditation are for us in order to resist his deceptions and attacks. "Satan leads many to believe that prayer to God is useless and but a form. He well knows how needful are meditation and prayer to keep Christ's followers aroused to resist his cunning and deception. By his devices he would divert the mind from these important exercises, that the soul may not lean for help upon the Mighty One and obtain strength from Him to resist his attacks."[8]

The disciples of Christ will be more successful and become stronger as they seek to spend time with God. The Bible reminds us to "be still, and know that I am God" (Psalm 46:10) because it is not easy to be still in this fast-paced world. We need to educate our minds to be still before the Lord.

Ellen White writes, "Educate your mind to love the Bible, to love the prayer meeting, to love the hour of meditation, and, above all, the hour when the soul communes with God. Become heavenly-minded if you would unite with the heavenly choir in the mansions above."[9]

We are warned not to neglect meditation and prayer, lest we lose religious interest and become careless. Ellen White writes, "God should be the highest object of our thoughts. Meditating upon him and pleading with Him elevate the soul and quicken the affections. A neglect of meditation and prayer will surely result in a declension in religious interests. Then will be seen carelessness and slothfulness."[10]

Lack of study and meditation leads the soul to spiritual dryness and joyless Christianity. Knowing the Bible is important. However, what is most important is the connection with God that we can get from studying the Word for personal devotion. Jesus said that eternal life depends mainly on the knowledge we can get of the Father and of Jesus Himself (John 17:3). And God has revealed Himself through the written Word.

TEN BENEFITS OF BIBLICAL MEDITATION

1. Brings peace of mind.

2. Elevates the soul and refines the mind.

3. Helps us to know our own hearts.

4. Increases moral strength.

5. Increases spiritual strength.

6. Prepares us to work for God.

7. Keeps us active and enthusiastic for God.

8. Resists the attacks and deceptions of the devil.

9. Provides strength and power from God.

10. Brings blessings from God according to His will.

ACTION STEPS

1. Take time this week to examine your prayer life.
2. Memorize Deuteronomy 6, following the outline for Ephesians 1 in the previous chapter.
3. As you repeat the verses, pray that God will show you how it applies in your life.
4. Set alarms, if need be, for specific times of prayer and meditation. And ask God to prompt you throughout the day to meditate on His Word and live in an attitude of prayer.
5. Pray Scripture. Here are some texts to get you started:
   a. "The Lord is near to all who call on him, to all who call on him in truth" (Psalm 145:18).
   b. "Call to me and I will answer you, and will tell you great and hidden things that you have not known" (Jeremiah 33:3, ESV).
   c. "Do not be anxious about anything, but in everything by prayer and supplication with thanksgiving let your request be made known to God. And the peace of God, which surpasses all understanding, will guard your hearts and your minds in Christ Jesus" (Philippians 4:6, 7, ESV).

Ask the Holy Spirit to help you memorize these beautiful promises.

BRINGS PEACE OF MIND.

Action: Spend quiet reflection on Philippians 4:7:
"And the peace of God, which transcends all understanding, will guard your hearts and your minds in Christ Jesus."

ELEVATES THE SOUL AND REFINES THE MIND.

Action: Meditate and pray Psalm 19:14:
"May these words of my mouth and this meditation of my heart be pleasing in your sight, Lord, my Rock and my Redeemer."

Helps us know our own hearts.

Action: Reflect deeply on Psalms 139:23:
"Search me, God, and know my heart; test me and know my anxious thoughts."

Increases moral strength.

Action: Contemplate in prayer Psalm 119:11:
"I have hidden your word in my heart that I might not sin against you."

Increases spiritual strength.

Action: Meditate on Ephesians 6:10:
"Finally, be strong in the Lord and in his mighty power."

Prepares us to work for God.

Action: Reflect on 2 Timothy 2:15:
"Do your best to present yourself to God as one approved, a worker who does not need to be ashamed and who correctly handles the word of truth."

Keeps us active and enthusiastic for God.

Action: Learn by memory Romans 12:11:
"Never be lacking in zeal, but keep your spiritual fervor, serving the Lord."

Helps us resist the attacks of the devil.

Action: Contemplate James 4:7:
"Submit yourselves, then, to God. Resist the devil, and he will flee from you."

Provides strength and power from God.

Action: Meditate on Isaiah 40:31:
"But those who hope in the Lord will renew their strength. They will soar on wings like eagles; they will run and not grow weary, they will walk and not be faint."

BRINGS SUCCESS AND PROSPERITY.

Action: Meditate on Joshua 1:8:

"Keep this Book of the Law always on your lips; meditate on it day and night, so that you may be careful to do everything written in it. Then you will be prosperous and successful."

ENDNOTES

[1]Edward McKendree Bounds, *The Complete Works of E. M. Bounds on Prayer: Experience the Wonders of God Through Prayer* (Grand Rapids: Baker Books, 2004), p. 143.

[2] Ellen G. White, *With God at Dawn* (Washington, D.C: Review and Herald Pub. Assn., 1949), p. 212.

[3]Ellen G. White, *Testimonies for the Church* (Mountain View, Calif.: Pacific Press Pub. Assn., 1948), vol. 3, p. 53.

[4]E. G. White, *With God at Dawn*, p. 213.

[5]Ellen G. White, *Education* (Mountain View, Calif.: Pacific Press Pub. Assn., 1903), p. 259.

[6]E. G. White, *Testimonies*, vol. 4, p. 459.

[7]*Ibid.*, vol. 1, p. 587.

[8]*Ibid.*, p. 295.

[9]*Ibid.*, vol. 2, p. 268.

[10]*Ibid.*, pp. 505, 506.

Chapter VII
Living the Memorized Word

"The Word of God is a great help in prayer.
If it be lodged and written in our hearts,
it will form an outflowing current of prayer,
full and irresistible."
—The Complete Works of E. M. Bounds on Prayer, p. 67

One night my family and I were attending a camp meeting in New Jersey when a terrifying incident awoke us. About 3:00 a.m. we suddenly heard a strange noise. To our dismay, we found out that our son, Gabriel, had fallen out of his bed and was convulsing violently on the floor. We were panicked and didn't know how to help him, so we immediately called 9-1-1 and waited anxiously for their arrival. It felt like an eternity.

Desperate and helpless, we turned to prayer, pleading with God for assistance. I said, "Lord, please send someone to help us." Amid our fear and uncertainty, we caught sight of the ambulance's lights piercing through the darkness from a distance. This moment led me to reflect on the scriptures that I had been memorizing, which was the book of Revelation. It felt as though God was reminding me of Revelation 19: help is on its way. The thought of Jesus coming back to rescue us gave us hope and comfort.

Learning scriptures by heart is a wonderful way to enhance our prayer life. Memorizing Scripture allows for a deeper understanding of its meaning. It can provide more profound insights during prayer, leading to a richer spiritual experience. When we have committed scriptures to memory, we can easily incorporate them into our prayers without a physical text. This accessibility means we can use Scripture to guide our prayers anytime and anywhere.

Understanding the dynamic between prayer and the Word of God is crucial for living a spirit-filled Christian life. E. M. Bounds wrote, "Here, let it be said, that no two things are more essential to a spirit-filled life than Bible reading and secret prayer; no two things more helpful to growth in grace; to getting the largest joy out of a Christian life; toward establishing one in the ways of eternal peace." And he warns us against neglecting these two essentials: "The neglect of these all-important duties presages leanness of soul, loss of joy, absence of peace, dryness of spirit, decay in all that pertains to spiritual life. Neglecting these things paves the way for apostasy and gives the evil one an advantage such as he is not likely to ignore."*

WHY PRAY WITH SCRIPTURE

Meditating in God's Word regularly and habitually, reciting the text we have learned back to Him in prayer, will strengthen our faith in God and help us live victoriously. As we talk with God in prayer, the Holy Spirit will bring to mind the exact text we need. For example, while praying for a challenging situation, I sometimes worry a little bit about finding a solution. It is at that precise moment that the Holy Spirit brings to my mind Philippians 4:6, 7: "Do not be anxious about anything, but in every situation, by prayer and petition, with thanksgiving, present your requests to God. And the peace of God, which transcends all understanding, will guard your hearts and your minds in Christ Jesus." And so the Spirit tells me, "It's OK. Everything will be fine. There is nothing to worry about; God will handle this situation." Then I pray that scripture and claim the promise.

In addition to strengthening our prayer lives, reciting memorized scriptures can help focus our minds during prayer, preventing distractions and fostering a more meaningful connection with God. Regularly reflecting on and praying the Bible can strengthen our faith and conviction. It reinforces the teachings and promises of our faith, making them more present and real in our lives. Additionally, memo-

84

rized scriptures can provide comfort and guidance, especially when we are distressed or uncertain. They can offer reassurance and direction in prayer and daily life.

Scripture can serve as a framework for our prayers, guiding us on what to pray for and how to approach, with a spiritual mindset, different situations. Integrating Scripture into our prayer life can help us feel closer to Jesus as we engage personally and intimately with the Bible texts and the teachings of Jesus. The discipline required to memorize Scripture can also foster a more disciplined prayer life. It encourages regular engagement with spiritual practices.

Having scriptures at the ready can be a powerful tool in moments of spiritual struggle. The truth and wisdom in the Word of God allow us to counter negative thoughts or temptations. By memorizing Bible texts, you can more easily relate your personal experiences to biblical teachings, seeing how the wisdom of the Scripture plays out in real life.

Incorporating memorized scriptures into your prayer life is not just about reciting words, but letting those words transform you. It's a practice that can lead to a more profound and enriching spiritual journey.

ACTION STEPS

Here are seven ways to incorporate scriptures into your daily life.

1. **READ:** "Blessed is he who reads and those who hear the words of this prophecy, and keep those things which are written in it; for the time is near" (Revelation 1:3, NKJV).
   - ➢ **Read every day the Bible text that you want to commit to memory.**

2. **LISTEN:** "So then faith comes by hearing, and hearing by the word of God" (Romans 10:17, NKJV).
   - ➢ **Listen to your Bible text before bed and upon waking.**

3. **STUDY:** "These were more fair-minded than those in Thessalonica, in that they received the word with all readiness, and searched the Scriptures daily to find out whether these things were so" (Acts 17:11, NKJV).
   - ➢ **Study the Bible text. Learn the keywords.**

4. MEMORIZE: "And these words which I command you today shall be in your heart" (Deuteronomy 6:6, NKJV).
  ➤ **Ask the Holy Spirit to help you put the text in your heart and mind.**

5. MEDITATE: "This Book of the Law shall not depart from your mouth, but you shall meditate in it day and night, that you may observe to do according to all that is written in it. For then you will make your way prosperous, and then you will have good success" (Joshua 1:8, NKJV).
  ➤ **Meditate on the text. Reflect on what God is telling you. Seek to obey.**

6. SHARE: "Go therefore and make disciples of all nations, baptizing them in the name of the Father and of the Son and of the Holy Spirit, teaching them to observe all that I have commanded you. And behold, I am with you always, to the end of the age" (Matthew 28:19, 20, ESV).
  ➤ **Share what you learn with others. Teach others the Word of God.**

7. ENJOY: "Oh, how I love Your law! It is my meditation all the day" (Psalm 119:97, NKJV).
  ➤ **Enjoy spending time with God and His Word. This brings eternal joy.**

PRAYER: "Dear God, help me to incorporate prayer and meditation into my daily life."

ENDNOTES

*Edward McKendree Bounds, *The Complete Works of E. M. Bounds on Prayer: Experience the Wonders of God Through Prayer* (Grand Rapids: Baker Books, 2004), p. 74.

Chapter VIII

The Transforming Power of the Bible

"How can a young man cleanse his way?
By taking heed according to Your word.
With my whole heart I have sought You;
Oh, let me not wander from Your commandments!
Your word I have hidden in my heart,
That I might not sin against You."
—Psalm 119:9-11, NKJV

When I was 16, a few friends and I went to a theater in New York City in order to watch an inappropriate movie, especially for my age. My friends were older, so they had no problem getting into the theater. However, I had to disguise myself. As a result, my mind was filled with sensual images that were difficult to erase.

After I gave my life to the Lord Jesus, was baptized, and joined the Seventh-day Adventist Church, I struggled with how to clean my mind. I asked God to help me, and He revealed to me Psalm 119:9. "How can a young man cleanse his way? By taking heed according to Your word" (NKJV). Since then I have been blessed beyond measure. In moments of temptation, sadness, or despair, the Holy Spirit brings to my memory the beautiful promises of the Bible. I have found comfort in many psalms, such as 23, 91, 100, 25, 19, 84, 122, 37, 34, and 8.

In addition, I have noticed that storing the Word of God in my mind has improved my memory. It's now easier for me to remember other things, because my brain constantly exercises its ability to memorize. The principle is true for us all. The more we exercise our minds, the sharper they become.

Memorizing the Word has also strengthened my faith. I am constantly listening to it in my mind. This makes sense because the Bible says, "Faith comes by hearing, and hearing by the word of God" (Romans 10:17, NKJV). The human mind is full of ideas, customs, images, habits, and ways of thinking. What we are and what we do is a direct result of our thoughts. Our experiences, customs, and beliefs—whether true or false—often shape our thoughts. Our social environment, fashion, people's opinions, and fears often shape our characters. Hence, it is essential to change our thinking. But to change how we think, we must change what we put into our minds.

In the Old Testament, God told His people that they should put God's words in their hearts. "And these words, which I command thee this day, shall be in thine heart: and thou shalt teach them diligently unto thy children, and shalt talk of them when thou sittest in thine house, and when thou walkest by the way, and when thou liest down, and when thou risest up" (Deuteronomy 6:6, 7, KJV). This is a commandment not only to memorize the Scriptures intellectually but to put them in the heart.

Knowing the Scriptures from the heart also helps us in our struggle against sin and the immoral inclinations of human nature. The Lord Jesus knew the Scriptures by heart. That is why, when the devil tempted Him, He could quote the words in the Old Testament. The disciples of the Lord Jesus also knew the Scriptures by heart. A clear example is Peter's message on the day of Pentecost (Acts 2:14-36). Also, Stephen's sermon before being stoned was given from memory (Acts 7:2-56).

There is little zeal and passion for the things of God in modern Christianity because we do not know the Word of God from the heart. If you want a change in your life, if you want to do something exciting, memorize a Bible verse each day. Your life will be transformed.

Maybe you think that it's too hard or that you don't have a good memory. But remember that we can do all things through Christ who strengthens us (Philippians 4:13). It may seem difficult at first, but as your mind gets used to the rigor of memorization, it will become easier and easier. Start with one verse per week. Then, one a day. Soon you will progress so much that you can memorize entire chapters in as little as a day.

METHODOLOGY FOR LEARNING THE BIBLE

My method to memorize the book of Revelation, Psalms, and many great passages of the Bible is simple: you must meditate on it and pray it.

All great feats in life begin with a first step. A spider's web is woven little by little. A mountain is climbed step by step. A chapter of the Bible is memorized verse by verse.

Suppose you want to start with this verse: "If ye abide in me, and my words abide in you, ye shall ask what ye will, and it shall be done unto you" (John 15:7, KJV). I would first break it down into natural phrases. For example:

1. If ye abide in me,

2. and my words abide in you,

3. ye shall ask what ye will,

4. and it shall be done unto you.

5. John 15:7, KJV

Repeat, "If ye abide in me," at least seven times three times a day. Ask God, "Lord, help me to abide in You. I want to abide in You. I don't want to leave Your presence for a minute. Keep me in Your presence. Don't ever turn away from me or allow me to turn away from You." This is a biblical prayer. When you pray this way, you will always remember those words. You will also be able to spend a long time praying without running out of words.

Next, repeat the second phrase seven times, "and my words remain in you," and pray, saying, "Lord, help me to put Your words in my heart so that I will not sin against You. Fill me with Your words. May Your words flow from my heart, and may I share Your wonders with others. Help me so that Your words remain in me."

Then repeat the phrase "ye shall ask what ye will," and pray, "Lord, fulfill Your promise in my life. I want to be filled with the Holy Spirit. I desire to be filled with wisdom. Bless my family. Transform my soul so that it may always serve you." You can ask for whatever you want at this point. It is a promise from God, and He always keeps His promises when we pray in His will. Ellen White reminds us, "We know that God hears us if we ask according to His will. But to press our petitions without a submissive spirit is not right; our prayers must take the form, not of command, but of intercession. . . . Our desires and interests should be lost in His will."[1]

Now repeat the last phrase: "and it shall be done unto you." Your request will be fulfilled. It is already a fact because He has promised it. He says that it shall be done unto you. He does not say maybe, or perhaps. These are categorical words: "it shall be done unto you." Ellen White observed, "The simple prayers indited by the Holy Spirit will ascent through the gates ajar, the open door which Christ has declared: I have opened, and no man can shut. These prayers, mingled with the incense of the perfection of Christ, will ascend as fragrance to the Father, and answers will come."[2] I have experienced this. God always hears my prayers and blesses me more than I deserve. God never fails.

Finally, you will have memorized John 15:7. Repeat it seven times until it becomes real in your mind. When you do this exercise, it is important to make it real and vivid. The more vivid, the more impact it will have. Use your imagination and, within your heart, contemplate God's words. They remain there. You feel happy because you are living according to God's will, and your prayers are answered.

Do you want to say to God right now, "Lord, help me so that I can have Your words in my heart"? If you pray that prayer, God will answer your prayer and transform your life.

ACTION STEPS

1. Ask the Holy Spirit which Bible text you should memorize.

2. Write it down, breaking it into natural phrases.

3. Repeat each phrase seven times, thinking about what that phrase tells you about God and how it can be applied to your life.

4. Pray according to each phrase that you repeat.

5. Repeat the biblical reference seven times, attaching it in your mind to the verse that you have learned.

ENDNOTES

[1] Ellen G. White, *The Faith I Live By* (Washington, D.C.: Review and Herald Pub. Assn., 1958), p. 315.

[2] Ellen G. White, *Testimonies for the Church* (Mountain View, Calif.: Pacific Press Pub. Assn., 1948), vol. 6, p. 467.

Chapter IX
The Power of Audio

"So then faith comes by hearing, and hearing by the word of God."
—Romans 10:17, NKJV

When my son Gabriel was about 3 or 4 years old, we purchased a book titled *First Steps*. This book also had an audio format that he would listen to every day. After a few days he had memorized the whole book, including the ding sounds that signaled a change of page. That is the power of audio. When I want to memorize a chapter from the Bible, I record that chapter and listen to it over and over until it becomes part of my memory.

The age-old tradition of memorizing the Bible is resurging in a digital era. People are turning to audio tools in order to aid memorization. Utilizing audio has numerous advantages; besides being highly convenient, it can have a significant impact on spiritual development.

Audio learning isn't just a modern convenience; it's a potent tool backed by science. Auditory processing plays a crucial role in how we absorb and recall information. Studies suggest listening can help us retain and comprehend information, particularly for auditory learners. When applied to scripture memorization, audio brings the Bible's narratives, teachings, and verses to life in a new and dynamic way.

The proliferation of audio Bibles has been a game changer. With many versions available—from dramatized renditions to straightforward narrations—people can now, through listening, absorb the Word of God. This method helps not only in memorizing verses but also in understanding the context and emotion behind the words, providing a more immersive experience.

Audio makes Scripture available almost anywhere. This is one of its greatest strengths. Busy schedules often leave little room for traditional study, but audio Bibles can be listened to during commutes, workouts, or household chores. This flexibility lets us engage with Scripture more frequently and consistently, embedding it deeper into our memories and daily lives.

The effectiveness of audio in memorizing the Bible is undeniable. It provides an easy, adaptable, and efficient way to internalize the Holy Scriptures. As technology advances, we are discovering new ways to engage with the Bible, making it easier to remember its timeless truths. By utilizing the power of audio, we can keep the Word of God close.

ACTION STEPS

I have been using audio to memorize the Bible for many years. Here is how you can maximize the benefits of memorizing the Bible using audio.

1. Find an app or recording device to record and play the recording in a loop. You will want to hear your Bible passage over and over. The app I use is called Wavepad.

2. Record the portion of the Bible that you want to memorize. You can read it yourself or use one of the audio Bibles available. I use "Faith Comes by Hearing." I record the Bible portion I want to memorize, and then play it over and over for as long as I want, in order to write the text on the tables of my heart.

3.   Use the same version of the Bible in audio as in writing.

4.   Listen to the audio when you go to bed.

5.   Listen when you get up in the morning.

6.   Listen while traveling by plane, car, train, or any mode of transportation.

Chapter X

How to Memorize an Entire Chapter

"And take the helmet of salvation,
and the sword of the Spirit,
which is the word of God."
—Ephesians 6:17, NKJV

After returning home from worship on a cold and rainy day in Oregon, I received a phone call from one of my church members. She was frantic, telling me how, after coming back from church, she found her husband dead. He had locked himself in the bathroom and shot himself.

I got in my car and headed over to her house. I had one thought in mind during my trip: "What am I going to say to this poor woman and her children? What words can bring comfort and peace in a moment like this?" Many things were swirling in my head, and I prayed that God would send His Holy Spirit to give me the right words. It was at that time that several Bible promises came to mind, and I was able to share them with the family to bring peace to their hearts in the midst of their sorrow.

When we fill our minds with the Word of God, the Holy Spirit will bring it back at the right moment to comfort others. My words do not have power to bring comfort and peace to a troubled heart. But the living, powerful Word of God, lodged in my heart, can be used by the Holy Spirit to touch people's lives. What a blessing we have to carry the Word of God in our hearts wherever we go!

So far, we have learned that the Holy Spirit is the key to Bible memorization. He will open our minds to understand the Scriptures, as He did for Jesus' disciples after the resurrection. Luke 24:45 says, "And He opened their understanding, that they might comprehend the Scriptures" (NKJV).

Additionally, we learned in Deuteronomy 6 that God gives us the secret to memorizing His Word. I call this method the secret of Bible memorization. So how can we apply the secret of Bible memorization to memorize an entire chapter we want to learn? Here is a suggestion:

1. Ask the Holy Spirit to help you choose a Bible text.

2. Pray for the Holy Spirit to help you memorize the text.

3. Read the text several times.

4. Record the text and listen to it as many times as possible.

5. Use your imagination. Think about the meaning. Think about the story in the text.

6. Write it down from memory.

7. Make a mental image of the Bible reference. See it in your mind. Do more than just say it—see it.

8. "Learn." Ask questions about the text. Ask the Holy Spirit to reveal what is happening in the story, who the main characters are, why the story was written, where and when it happened, and what the context is.

9. "Obey." Ask God for help in applying the teachings to your life. Follow what you learn.

10. "Teach." Become a disciple maker. Teach other people what you learn in the Bible. The best way to learn something is to teach it. And that is how you make disciples around the world. Use the principle of 2 Timothy 2:2.

11. "Repeat." Repeat this process over and over until it is impressed in the heart.

12. "Talk." Share the Word of God all the time. Speak about His works, His words, and His love. Share the Bible text you are learning.

13. "Bind." Create an emotional and psychological bond with the texts. Become completely absorbed by the text you are committing to memory. Bond with the text.

14. "Write." Ask the Holy Spirit to help you carve the text into your heart.

Once you have gone through this process, you will not likely forget what you have learned. And even if it fades from your mind a little, the Holy Spirit will remind you of the text at the appropriate time.

ACTION STEPS

Memorize the first chapters of Ephesians, Philippians, and Colossians using this methodology. See Appendixes A, B, and D for the outlines for memorizing each chapter. In these appendixes I employ italics, boldface type, and underlining to aid in easily remembering each sentence.

Chapter XI
Always Be Ready to Witness

"But sanctify the Lord God in your hearts, and always be ready to give a defense to everyone who asks you a reason for the hope that is in you,
with meekness and fear; having a good conscience, that when they defame you as evildoers, those who revile your good conduct in Christ may be ashamed."
—1 Peter 3:15, 16, NKJV

A few years ago I went to a hospital for surgery. I have always been blessed with good health and have never spent much time in a hospital. However, this time was different. I found myself not wanting to leave the hospital, and even wished to spend a few more days there.

It's not common for anyone to want to stay in a hospital longer than necessary, but in my case I did. Can you guess why? Here's a hint: it wasn't because of the food. And it wasn't because I was sick. No, I was perfectly fine. I needed to stay in the hospital for only one night. But I believe I had a divine appointment at that hospital. I went to the hospital at 5:30 in the morning. My surgery was at 7:30 a.m. When I woke up from the anesthesia, a nurse was standing in front of my bed. I was kind of groggy and tired from the surgery. But she began to talk with me.

"How are you feeling?" she asked.

"I am in pain, but otherwise I feel great," I replied.

"Do you smoke?"

"No."

"Do you use drugs?"

"No."

"Do you drink?"

"Yes, I am a heavy drinker," I replied.

She looked at me surprised, but I quickly added, "I do not drink alcohol, but I drink a lot of water because water is a powerful remedy. Do you know that water is one of the eight powerful secrets for good health and longevity? Did you know about this?"

"No, I didn't," she responded.

"Because you are in the health profession, it will be good for you to know this. I am going to share the eight powerful principles of health."

So I briefly talked about nutrition, exercise, water, sunshine, temperance, air, rest, and trust in God. When I spoke about trust in God, I began to share Bible promises. The Holy Spirit reminded me of Christ's promises. For example, I shared with her Isaiah 26:3: "You will keep him in perfect peace, whose mind is stayed on You, because he trusts in You" (NKJV).

The Bible says that those who trust God will have perfect peace. As I began to share these beautiful promises, I could see her eyes welling up with tears. Soon they flowed. I could see her face mask getting wet. And I just kept sharing promises.

Then she said: "You don't know how much I need this. I am so glad you are talking to me about this."

She shared with me that two weeks ago she had lost her husband. He was an expert swimmer, but had tragically passed away from a heart attack while swimming. She blamed herself because she hadn't accompanied him to the river and felt she should have been there with him. I then started to share more Bible promises with her.

Some of those promises were "But our citizenship is in heaven. And we eagerly await a Savior from there, the Lord Jesus Christ, who, by the power that enables him to bring everything under his control, will transform our lowly bodies so that they will be like his glorious body" (Philippians 3:20, 21).

"Do not be anxious about anything, but in everything by prayer and supplication with thanksgiving let your requests be made known to God. And the peace of God, which surpasses all understanding, will guard your hearts and minds in Christ Jesus" (Philippians 4:6, 7, ESV).

We spent what seemed like one hour talking, and at the end she said, "This is not fair; I am supposed to be taking care of you."

She had forgotten my pain medicine. And I had forgotten my pain.

"Don't worry," I said. "My wound will heal, and my pain will go away. The important thing is that God sent me to this hospital to tell you how important you are to Him and how much He loves you."

MEMORIZING FOR OUTREACH

As I thought about this experience, I couldn't help reflecting, again, on the importance of internalizing the Word of God. More than just as a practice of faith, storing the Word of God in our minds can be a means of comfort, hope, and guidance to others, especially when physical Bibles cannot be accessed or read.

This experience also underscores the role of the Holy Spirit. He helps us recall what we have memorized in order to share the living water of God's Word, even in moments of personal adversity. This aligns with the biblical encouragement in Psalm 119:11: "I have hidden your word in my heart that I might not sin against you." This verse speaks to the protective and expressive power of internalized Scripture.

God wants to have an intimate relationship with you. And through you He wants to bless others. I don't understand how the God of the universe, who created the heavens and the earth, wants to have a close, intimate relationship with me. It is beyond my comprehension. I just accept by faith that it is true. God wants to spend quality time with us. That can be explained only by the great love with which He loves us. As Paul wrote in Ephesians 2:4-8: "But God, who is rich in mercy, because of His great love with which He loved us, even when we were dead in trespasses, made us alive together with Christ (by grace you have been saved), and raised us up together, and made us sit together in the heavenly places in Christ Jesus, that in the ages to come He might show the exceeding riches of His grace in His kindness toward us in Christ Jesus. For by grace you have been saved through faith, and that not of yourselves; it is the gift of God" (NKJV).

God is rich in mercy. His love is great. He made us alive, raised us up with Christ, and made us sit together with Christ in heaven. His grace is exceedingly abundant, and He is kind toward us. He has given us the gift of salvation in Christ Jesus. I praise God for His incredible love.

According to Psalm 1, the difference between the righteous and the wicked lies in what they meditate on. The righteous dwell on the Word of God, His actions, and His teachings, while the wicked fixate on their sinful desires and deeds. This theme underscores the notion that our thoughts and actions are closely intertwined.

To reshape our minds, we must change the content we fill them with. The Bible emphasizes that God's people should cherish His words in their hearts: "And these words, which I command thee this day, shall be in thine heart" (Deuteronomy 6:6, KJV). This command encourages more than a mere intellectual grasp of the Scriptures—it urges us to treasure them in our hearts, reflecting a profound internalization of God's word. When we learn, and then contemplate, the words, they become part of our natures.

This Old Testament emphasis continues throughout the New Testament, where Paul advises the Colossian church, "Let the word of Christ dwell in you richly in all wisdom, teaching and admonishing one another in psalms and hymns and spiritual songs, singing with grace in your hearts to the Lord" (Colossians 3:16, KJV).

Memorizing Scripture helps strengthen cognitive ability, making our minds sharper as a result, and helping us develop the mind of Christ. Ellen G. White says, "The Bible is the best book in the world for giving intellectual culture. Its study taxes the mind, strengthens the memory, and sharpens the intellect more than the study of all the subjects that human philosophy embraces."*1

Memorizing the Word of God provides spiritual strength in our battle against sin and our corrupt nature. Jesus, with His intimate knowledge of the Scriptures, could quote from the Old Testament, when tempted by Satan (Matthew 4:1-11). His disciples, too, showed deep scriptural knowledge in their sermons (Acts 2:14-36, Acts 7:2-56). Such examples demonstrate the transformative power of internalizing the Scriptures. Sadly, we often lack the passion seen in these biblical examples, largely because we fail to internalize God's Word.

SCRIPTURE AS PRAYER

Consider transforming each verse into a prayer as a practical method for internalizing the Word of God. This approach allows the Scripture to be deeply ingrained in your heart, creating a profound bond with the Word of God.

The repetition of a Bible verse or chapter, coupled with asking God to send His Holy Spirit to guide the memorization process, helps to deeply engrave the verse into the mind and heart. Remember, the Holy Spirit is key to memorization.

According to Deuteronomy 6, we must learn, obey, teach, repeat, talk, bind, and write the Word of God in our hearts every day. But mere memorization is not the goal. We need to seek to understand the will of God. We ask the Holy Spirit to help us understand each Bible verse, and He will. We will always remember what we understand because we gain spiritual understanding.

Regarding matters of spirituality, the human mind, sculpted and enlightened by the Word of God, as expressed in Ephesians 1:18, maintains an indisputable superiority. Immerse yourself in the Scriptures in order to acquire spiritual intelligence from God. It is time to go back to the Bible and study it like never before, writing the beautiful words of God in our hearts. Would you ask the Holy Spirit to help you memorize His words? The action step for this chapter is a challenge for you and me:

ACTION STEPS

1. Remember to ask for and receive a fresh baptism of the Holy Spirit daily.
2. Develop the habit of consistently memorizing Bible verses daily.
3. Review the Bible texts you have already learned daily.
4. Consistently teach what you learned to others.

ENDNOTES

*Ellen G. White. *Gospel Workers* (Washington, D.C.: Review and Herald Pub. Assn., 1915), p. 100.

Appendix A
Outline for Memorizing Ephesians 1

Notice how the Holy Spirit helps you remember the words. With this chapter I am using the New King James Version. I have used numerous aids (boldface type, underlining, etc.) to help in remembering each sentence.

EPHESIANS 1

SECTION 1: EPHESIANS 1:1-6—BIBLICAL METHODOLOGY

1. <u>Paul</u>, an apostle of Jesus Christ by the will of God,

   To the saints who are in Ephesus,

   and faithful in Christ Jesus:

2. <u>Grace to you</u> and peace from God our Father and the Lord Jesus Christ.

3. **<u>Blessed be the</u> God and Father of our Lord Jesus Christ,**

   who has blessed us with every spiritual blessing in the heavenly places in Christ,

4. **<u>just as He chose us</u> in Him before the foundation of the world,**

   that we should be holy and without blame before Him in love,

5. having <u>predestined</u> us to adoption as sons by Jesus Christ to Himself,

   according to the good pleasure of His will,

6. *<u>to the praise</u> of the glory of His grace,*

   by which He made us accepted in the Beloved.

Repeat these six Bible verses until they are clear in your mind.

To remember the Bible reference, make mental image of the number as you repeat the text.

Section 2: Ephesians 1:7-12

7. In Him we have redemption through His blood,

    the forgiveness of sins, according to the riches of His grace

8. *which He made to abound toward us in all wisdom and prudence,*

9. **having made known to us the mystery of His will,**

    according to His good pleasure which He purposed in
    Himself,

10. that in the dispensation of the fullness of the times He
    might **gather together** in one all things in Christ,
    both which are in heaven and which are on earth—in Him.

11. **In Him also we have obtained an inheritance,**
    being predestined according to the purpose of Him who
    works all things according to the counsel of His will,

12. **that we who first trusted in Christ should be to the**
    praise of His glory.

Now combine with the first six verses and repeat.

Section 3: Ephesians 1:13-18

13. In Him you also trusted, after you heard the word of truth,
    the gospel of your salvation;
    in whom also, having believed, you were sealed with the
    Holy Spirit of promise,

14. who is the guarantee of our inheritance until the redemption of
    the purchased possession, to the praise of His glory.

15. ***Therefore*** **I also, after I heard of your faith in the Lord**
    Jesus and your love for all the saints,

16. do not cease to give thanks for you, making mention of you
in my prayers:
17. *that the God of our Lord Jesus Christ, the Father of glory,*
may give to you the spirit of wisdom and revelation in
the knowledge of Him,
18. **the eyes of your understanding being enlightened;**
that you may know what is the hope of His
calling, what are the riches of the glory of His
inheritance in the saints,

Do the same thing here: Add these with the first 12 verses and repeat.

Section 4: Ephesians 1:19-23

19. **and** what is the exceeding greatness of His power toward us
who believe, according to the working of His mighty power
20. *which He worked in Christ when* **He raised Him** *from the*
dead and **seated Him** *at His right hand in the heavenly places,*
21. **far above all**
principality
and power
and might
and dominion,
and **every name** that is named, not only in this age but also
in that which is to come.
22. **And He put all things under His feet,**
and gave Him to be head over all things to the church,
23. *which is His body, the fullness of Him who fills all in all.*

Repeat these verses, from 1 to 23, until they are clear in your
mind. To remember the Bible reference, make a mental image of
the verse number as you repeat the text.

Appendix B

Outline for Memorizing Philippians 1

With Philippians I am using the New International Version.

PHILIPPIANS 1

Section 1: Philippians 1:1-6—Biblical Methodology

1. Paul and Timothy,

   servants of Christ Jesus,

   To all God's holy people in Christ Jesus at Philippi,

   together with the overseers and deacons:

2. **Grace and peace to you from God our Father and the Lord Jesus Christ.**

3. I thank my God every time I remember you.

4. **In all my prayers for all of you, I always pray with joy**

5. *because of your partnership in the gospel from the first day until now,*

6. being confident of this, that he who began a good work in you will carry it on to completion until the day of Christ Jesus.

Section 2: Philippians 1:7-11

7. **It is right for me to feel this way about all of you,**

   since I have you in my heart and,

   whether I am in chains or defending and confirming the gospel,

   all of you share in God's grace with me.

8. *God can testify how I long for all of you with the affection of Christ Jesus.*

9. **And this is my prayer:**
   that your love may abound more and more in knowledge and depth of insight,

10. *so that you may be able to discern what is best*
    and may be pure and blameless for the day of Christ,

11. **filled with the fruit of righteousness that comes through Jesus Christ—**
    to the glory and praise of God.

SECTION 3: PHILIPPIANS 1:12-16

12. Now I want you to know, brothers and sisters,
    that what has happened to me has <u>actually served</u> to advance the gospel.

13. *As a result, it has become clear throughout the whole palace guard* **and to everyone else that I am in chains for Christ.**

14. And because of my chains,
    most of the brothers and sisters have become confident in the Lord
    and dare **all the more** to proclaim the gospel without fear.

15. It is true that some preach Christ out of envy and rivalry,
    but others out of goodwill.

16. The latter do so out of love,
    knowing that I am put here for the defense of the gospel.

SECTION 4: PHILIPPIANS 1:17-21

17. *The former preach Christ out of selfish ambition, not sincerely,*
    supposing that they can stir up trouble for me while I am in chains.

18. **But what does it matter?**
    The important thing is that in every way, whether from false motives or true,
    Christ is preached. And because of this I rejoice.
    Yes, and I will continue to rejoice,

19. for I know that through your prayers

    and God's provision of the Spirit of Jesus Christ

    what has happened to me will turn out for my deliverance.

20. I eagerly expect and hope that I will in no way be ashamed,

    but will have sufficient courage

    so that now as always Christ will be exalted in my body,

    whether by life or by death.

21. *For to me, to live is Christ and to die is gain.*

Section 5: Philippians 1:22-26

22. If I am to go on living in the body, this will mean fruitful labor for me.

    Yet what shall I choose?

    I do not know!

23. *I am torn between the two:*

    I desire to depart and be with Christ,

    which is better by <u>far</u>;

24. but it is more necessary for you that I remain in the body.

25. Convinced of this, I know that I will remain,

    and I will continue with all of you for your progress

    and joy in the faith,

26. *so that through my being with you again*

    your boasting in Christ Jesus will abound on account of me.

Section 6: Philippians 1:27-30

27. *Whatever happens,*

    conduct yourselves in a manner worthy of the gospel of Christ.

    Then, whether I come and see you or only hear about you in my absence,

    I will know that you stand firm in the one Spirit,

    striving together as one for the faith of the gospel

28. *without being frightened in any way by those who oppose you.*
    This is a sign to them that they will be destroyed,
    but that you will be saved—and that by God.

29. *For it has been granted to you on behalf of Christ not only to believe in him,*
    but <u>also</u> to suffer for him,

30. *since you are going through the same struggle you saw I had,*
    and now hear that I still have.

Appendix C
Sample Memorization Schedule for Philippians 1

Because Philippians 1 has 30 verses, a manageable approach would be to memorize one verse per day, giving yourself a few days for review and reflection. Here's a five-week plan.

Week 1: Verses 1-7

- ➤ **Day 1**: Philippians 1:1
- ➤ **Day 2**: Philippians 1:2
- ➤ **Day 3**: Philippians 1:3
- ➤ **Day 4**: Philippians 1:4
- ➤ **Day 5**: Philippians 1:5
- ➤ **Day 6**: Philippians 1:6
- ➤ **Day 7**: Review Verses 1-6

Week 2: Verses 7-12

- ➤ **Day 8**: Philippians 1:7
- ➤ **Day 9**: Philippians 1:8
- ➤ **Day 10**: Philippians 1:9
- ➤ **Day 11**: Philippians 1:10
- ➤ **Day 12**: Philippians 1:11
- ➤ **Day 13**: Philippians 1:12
- ➤ **Day 14**: Review Verses 7-12

Week 3: Verses 13-18

- ➢ **Day 15**: Philippians 1:13
- ➢ **Day 16**: Philippians 1:14
- ➢ **Day 17**: Philippians 1:15
- ➢ **Day 18**: Philippians 1:16
- ➢ **Day 19**: Philippians 1:17
- ➢ **Day 20**: Philippians 1:18
- ➢ **Day 21**: Review Verses 13-18

Week 4: Verses 19-24

- ➢ **Day 22**: Philippians 1:19
- ➢ **Day 23**: Philippians 1:20
- ➢ **Day 24**: Philippians 1:21
- ➢ **Day 25**: Philippians 1:22
- ➢ **Day 26**: Philippians 1:23
- ➢ **Day 27**: Philippians 1:24
- ➢ **Day 28**: Review Verses 19-24

Week 5: Verses 25-30 and Final Review

- ➢ **Day 29**: Philippians 1:25
- ➢ **Day 30**: Philippians 1:26
- ➢ **Day 31**: Philippians 1:27
- ➢ **Day 32**: Philippians 1:28
- ➢ **Day 33**: Philippians 1:29
- ➢ **Day 34**: Philippians 1:30
- ➢ **Day 35**: Final Review of Philippians 1:1-30

Each day, follow these steps:

1. **Read the verse out loud**: Read the verse several times, out loud if possible.

2. **Write the verse**: Write the verse down in a notebook or on a note card.

3. **Recite the verse**: Recite the verse from memory throughout the day.

4. **Reflect on the meaning**: Consider what the verse means and how it applies to your life.

5. **Review previous verses**: Meditate on the verse.

    What is God telling you in this verse?

Spend a few minutes reviewing the verses memorized in previous days. Make a vivid image in your mind about the text. Remember, the goal of memorizing Scripture is not just to recall the words but to meditate on their meaning and integrate their teachings into your life.

Appendix D

Outline for Memorizing Colossians 1

Again, I am using the New International Version.

COLOSSIANS 1

SECTION 1: COLOSSIANS 1:1-6—BIBLICAL METHODOLOGY

1. *Paul, an apostle of Christ Jesus by the will of God, and Timothy our brother,*

2. **To God's holy people in Colossae,**

   the faithful brothers and sisters in Christ:

   Grace and peace to you from God our Father.

3. We always thank God,

   the Father of our Lord Jesus Christ,

   when we pray for you,

4. because we have heard of your faith in Christ Jesus

   and of the love you have for all God's people—

5. the faith and love that spring from the hope stored up for you in heaven

   and about which you have already heard in the true message of the gospel

6. **that has come to you.**

   In the same way,

   the gospel is bearing fruit and growing throughout the whole world—

   just as it has been doing among you

   since the day you heard it

   and truly understood God's grace.

Section 2: Colossians 1:7-12

7.   You learned it from Epaphras, our dear fellow servant,
   who is a faithful minister of Christ on our behalf,

8.   and who also told us of your love in the Spirit.

9.   **For this reason, since the day we heard about you,**
   we have not stopped praying for you.
   We continually ask God to fill you with the knowledge of his will
   through all the wisdom and understanding that the Spirit gives,

10. **so that you may live a life worthy of the Lord**
    and please him in every way:
    bearing fruit in every good work,
    growing in the knowledge of God,

11. being strengthened with all power according to his glorious might
    so that you may have great endurance and patience,

12. **and giving joyful thanks to the <u>Father</u>,**
    who has qualified you to share in the inheritance of his holy people
    in the kingdom of light.

Section 3: Colossians 1:13-17

13.   For he has rescued us from the dominion of darkness
    and brought us into the kingdom of the Son he loves,

14.   in whom we have redemption, the forgiveness of sins.

15. *The Son is the image of the invisible God, the firstborn over all
    creation.*

16. **For in him all things were created:**
    things in heaven and on earth,
    visible and invisible,
    whether thrones or powers or rulers or <u>authorities</u>;
    all things have been created through him and for him.

17. He is before all things,
    and in him all things hold together.

SECTION 4: COLOSSIANS 1:18-23

18. **And he is the head of the body, the church;**
    he is the beginning and the firstborn from among the dead,
    so that in everything he might have the supremacy.
19. For God was pleased to have all his fullness dwell in him,
20. *and through him to reconcile to himself all things, whether
    things on earth or things*
    in heaven, by making peace through his blood, shed on the cross.
21. **Once you were alienated from God**
    and were enemies in your minds because of your evil behavior.
22. But now he has reconciled you by Christ's physical body
    through death to present you holy in his sight,
    without blemish and free from accusation—
23. if you continue in your faith,
    established and firm,
    and do not move from the hope held out in the gospel.
    This is the gospel that you heard
    and that has been proclaimed to every creature under heaven,
    and of which I, Paul, have become a servant.

SECTION 5: COLOSSIANS 1:24-29

24. **Now I rejoice in what I am suffering for you,**
    and I fill up in my flesh what is still lacking in regard to Christ's afflictions,
    for the sake of his body, which is the church.
25. **I have become its servant by the commission**
    God gave me to present to you the word of God in its fullness—

26. *the mystery that has been kept hidden for ages and generations,*
    but is now disclosed to the Lord's people.

27. To them God has chosen to make known among the Gentiles
    the glorious riches of this mystery,
    which is Christ in you, the hope of glory.

28. **He is the one we proclaim,**
    admonishing and teaching everyone with all wisdom,
    so that we may present everyone fully mature in Christ.

29. To this end I strenuously contend with all the energy Christ
    so powerfully works in me.

Appendix E

Ellen G. White Statements on Memorizing the Bible

1. COMMIT TO MEMORY TEXT AFTER TEXT:

"God's precious Word is the standard for youth who would be loyal to the King of heaven. Let them study the Scriptures. Let them commit text after text to memory, and acquire a knowledge of what the Lord has said" (*My Life Today* [Washington, D.C.: Review and Herald Pub. Assn., 1952], p. 315).

2. BUILD A WALL OF SCRIPTURES AROUND YOU:

"Build a wall of scriptures around you, and you will see that the world cannot break it down. Commit the Scriptures to memory, and then throw right back upon Satan when he comes with his temptations, 'It is written.' This is the way that our Lord met the temptations of Satan, and resisted them" (in *Review and Herald*, Apr. 10, 1888).

3. HANG IN MEMORY'S HALL THE PRECIOUS WORDS OF CHRIST:

"Hang in memory's hall the precious words of Christ. They are to be valued far above silver or gold" (*Testimonies for the Church* [Mountain View, Calif.: Pacific Press Pub. Assn., 1948], vol. 6, p. 81).

4. TAKE ADVANTAGE OF EVERY OPPORTUNITY TO MEMORIZE THE BIBLE:

"Keep a pocket Bible with you as you work, and improve every opportunity to commit to memory its precious promises" (in *Review and Herald*, Apr. 27, 1905).

5. MEMORIZE THE WORD OF GOD SO THAT NO ONE CAN TAKE AWAY FROM YOU:

"The time will come when many will be deprived of the written Word. But if this Word is printed in the memory, no one can take it from us" (*Manuscript Releases* [Silver Spring, Md.: Ellen G. White Estate, 1993], vol. 20, p. 64].

6. COMMIT TO MEMORY IMPORTANT PASSAGES:

"Let the more important passages of Scripture . . . be committed to memory. . . . Though at first the memory may be defective, it will gain strength by exercise, so that after a time you will delight thus to treasure up the precious words of truth" (*Counsels on Sabbath School Work* (Washington, D.C.: Review and Herald Pub. Assn., 1938), p. 42].

7. RECEIVE PROTECTION AGAINST THE ENEMY:

"We must be better acquainted with our Bibles. We might close the door to many temptations, if we would commit to memory passages of Scripture. Let us hedge up the way to Satan's temptations with 'It is written.'" (*God's Amazing Grace* [Washington, D.C.: Review and Herald Pub. Assn., 1973], p. 262, emphasis added).

8. MEMORIZE BIBLE PROMISES:

"Study the Word of God. Commit its precious promises to memory so that, when we shall be deprived of our Bibles, we may still be in possession of the Word of God" (*Last Day Events* [Boise, Idaho: Pacific Press Pub. Assn., 1992], pp. 67, 68).

9. FILL THE MIND WITH PRECIOUS TRUTH:

"Truth must be graven on the tablets of the soul. The memory must be filled with the precious truths of the Word. Then, like beautiful gems, these truths will flash out in the life" (*Messages to Young People* [Nashville: Southern Pub. Assn., 1930], p. 69).

10. GOD WILL HELP YOU REMEMBER WHAT YOU LEARNED:

"God will flash the knowledge obtained by diligent searching of the Scriptures into their memory at the very time when it is needed. But if they neglect to fill their minds with the gems of truth, if they do not acquaint themselves with the words of Christ, if they have never tasted the power of His grace in trial, then they cannot expect that the Holy Spirit will bring His words to their remembrance. They are to serve God daily with their undivided affections, and then trust Him" (*Testimonies on Sabbath School Work* [Washington, D.C.: Review and Herald Pub. Assn., 1900], p. 106).

11. USE IMAGES TO HELP MEMORIZE THE WORD:

"The use of object lessons, blackboards, maps, and pictures will be an aid in explaining these lessons, and fixing them in the memory. Parents and teachers should constantly seek for improved methods. The teaching of the Bible should have our freshest thought, our best methods, and our most earnest effort" (*Education* [Mountain View, Calif.: Pacific Press Pub. Assn., 1903], p. 186).

12. THE BIBLE IS THE BEST BOOK FOR STRENGTHENING THE MIND:

"The Bible is the best book in the world for giving intellectual culture. Its study taxes the mind, strengthens the memory, and sharpens the intellect more than the study of all the subjects that human philosophy embraces. The great themes which it presents, the dignified simplicity with which these themes are handled, the light which is shed upon the great problems of life, bring strength and vigor to the understanding" (*Gospel Workers* [Washington, D.C.: Review and Herald Pub. Assn., 1915], p. 100).

13. THE WALDENSES KNEW LARGE PORTIONS OF THE OLD AND NEW TESTAMENTS:

"Many were able to repeat large portions of both the Old and the New Testament. Thoughts of God were associated alike with the sublime scenery of nature and with the humble blessings of daily life. Little children learned to look with gratitude to God as the giver of every favor and every comfort" (*The Great*

Controversy [Mountain View, Calif.: Pacific Press Pub. Assn., 1911], p. 67).

14. THEY MEMORIZED MATTHEW AND JOHN AND MANY EPISTLES:

"From their pastors the youth received instruction. While attention was given to branches of general learning, the Bible was made the chief study. The Gospels of Matthew and John were committed to memory, with many of the Epistles. They were employed also in copying the Scriptures. Some manuscripts contained the whole Bible, others only brief selections, to which some simple explanations of the text were added by those who were able to expound the Scriptures. Thus were brought forth the treasures of truth so long concealed by those who sought to exalt themselves above God" (*The Great Controversy* [Mountain View, Calif.: Pacific Press Pub. Assn., 1911], pp. 68, 69).

15. PORTIONS OF SCRIPTURE, EVEN WHOLE CHAPTERS, MAY BE COMMITTED TO MEMORY:

"The mind must be restrained and not allowed to wander. It should be trained to dwell upon the Scriptures and upon noble, elevating themes. Portions of Scripture, even whole chapters, may be committed to memory to be repeated when Satan comes in with his temptations" (*Mind, Character, and Personality* [Nashville: Southern Pub. Assn., 1977], vol. 1, p. 95).

16. SEVERAL TIMES EACH DAY A BIBLE TEXT SHOULD BE COMMITTED TO MEMORY:

"Several times each day precious, golden moments should be consecrated to prayer and the study of the Scriptures, if it is only to commit a text to memory, that spiritual life may exist in the soul. The varied interests of the cause furnish us with food for reflection and inspiration for our prayers. Communion with God is highly essential for spiritual health, and here only may be obtained that wisdom and correct judgment so necessary in the performance of every duty" (*Testimonies for the Church* [Mountain View, Calif.: Pacific Press Pub. Assn., 1948), vol. 4, p. 459).

17. MEMORIZE THE BIBLE AT EVERY OPPORTUNITY:

"Keep your Bible with you. As you have opportunity, read it; fix the texts in your memory. Even while you are walking the streets, you may read a passage, and meditate upon it, thus fixing it in the mind" (*Christian Education* [Battle Creek, Mich.: International Tract Society, 1893], p. 58).

18. MINISTERS NEED TO MEMORIZE PORTIONS OF THE BIBLE:

"Ministers should devote time to reading, to study, to meditation and prayer. They should store the mind with useful knowledge, committing to memory portions of Scripture, tracing out the fulfilment of the prophecies, and learning the lessons which Christ gave His disciples. Take a book with you to read when traveling on the cars or waiting in the railway station. Employ every spare moment in doing something. In this way an effectual door will be closed against a thousand temptations" (*Gospel Workers* [Washington, D.C.: Review and Herald Pub. Assn., 1915], p. 278).

Appendix F

List of Bible Chapters and Verses Recommended by Ellen White for Study in These Last Days

The following is a list of Bible chapters and texts recommended by Ellen G. White to prepare for Jesus' second coming.

"The mind must be restrained, and not allowed to wander. It should be trained to dwell upon the Scriptures; **even whole chapters may be committed to memory, to be repeated when Satan comes with his temptations**. Even while you are walking on the streets, you may read a passage and meditate upon it, thus fixing it in your mind, and God will flash the knowledge obtained into the memory at the very time when it is needed" (in *West Michigan Herald*, Oct. 26, 1904).

"Portions of Scripture, even whole chapters, may be committed to memory, to be repeated when Satan comes in with his temptations. . . . When Satan would lead the mind to dwell upon earthly and sensual things, he is most effectually resisted with, 'It is written'" (*Mind, Character, and Personality* [Nashville: Southern Pub. Assn., 1977], p. 659).

1. Exodus 20

"Evening and morning join with your children in God's worship, reading His Word and singing His praise. Teach them to repeat God's law" (*Evangelism* [Washington, D.C.: Review and Herald Pub. Assn., 1946], p. 499).

2. DEUTERONOMY 30

"The more deeply to impress these truths upon all minds, the great leader embodied them in sacred verse. This song was not only historical, but prophetic. While it recounted the wonderful dealings of God with His people in the past, it also foreshadowed the great events of the future, the final victory of the faithful when Christ shall come the second time in power and glory. The people were directed to commit to memory this poetic history, and to teach it to their children and children's children. It was to be chanted by the congregation when they assembled for worship, and to be repeated by the people as they went about their daily labors. It was the duty of parents to so impress these words upon the susceptible minds of their children that they might never be forgotten" (*Patriarchs and Prophets* [Mountain View, Calif.: Pacific Press Pub. Assn., 1890, 1908], pp. 467, 468).

3. PSALM 19

"We would do well to read often the nineteenth psalm that we may understand how the Lord binds up His law with His created works" (*The Seventh-day Adventist Bible Commentary*, Ellen G. White Comments [Washington, D.C.: Review and Herald Pub. Assn., 1954], vol. 3, p. 1143).

4. PSALMS 105 AND 106

"The experience of Israel, referred to in the above words by the apostle, and as recorded in the one hundred fifth and one hundred sixth psalms, contains lessons of warning that the people of God in these last days especially need to study. I urge that these chapters be read at least once every week" (*Testimonies to Ministers* [Mountain View, Calif.: Pacific Press Pub. Assn., 1923], pp. 98, 99).

5. ISAIAH 51

"The whole of the fifty-first chapter of Isaiah is worthy of close, earnest study, and we would do well to **commit it to memory.**

It has a special application to those who are living in the last days" (in *Review and Herald*, Dec. 1, 1896).

6. Isaiah 53

"Prophecy foretold that Christ was to appear as a root out of dry ground. 'He hath no form nor comeliness,' wrote Isaiah, 'and when we shall see him, there is no beauty that we should desire him. He is despised and rejected of men; a man of sorrows, and acquainted with grief: and we hid as it were our faces from him; he was despised, and we esteemed him not.' **This chapter should be studied.** It presents Christ as the Lamb of God. Those who are lifted up with pride, whose souls are filled with vanity, should look upon this picture of their Redeemer, and humble themselves in the dust. **The entire chapter should be committed to memory.** Its influence will subdue and humble the soul defiled by sin and uplifted by self-exaltation" (in *The Youth's Instructor*, Dec. 20, 1900, emphasis added).

7. Isaiah 58

"The mind must be restrained, and not allowed to wander. It **should be trained to dwell upon the Scriptures**; even whole chapters may be committed to memory, to be repeated when Satan comes in with his temptations. **The fifty-eighth of Isaiah is a profitable chapter for this purpose**" (*Gospel Workers* [Battle Creek, Mich.: Review and Herald Pub. Co., 1892], p. 418, emphasis added).

8. John 13, 14, 15, 16, and 17

"I feel intensely when I read and dwell upon the subjects contained in the **13th, 14th, 15th, 16th, and 17th chapters of John. These lessons are of deep import and need to be studied and even committed to memory**" (Ellen G. White manuscript 42, 1890, in *Letters and Manuscripts* [Silver Spring, Md.: Ellen G. White Estate], vol. 6, p. 308).

9. John 17

"Study prayerfully the seventeenth chapter of John. **This chapter is not only to be read again and again; its truths are to be eaten and assimilated**" (*Testimonies for the Church* [Mountain View, Calif.: Pacific Press Pub. Assn., 1948], vol. 8, p. 80, emphasis added).

10. 1 Corinthians 12 and 13

"The twelfth and thirteenth chapters of 1 Corinthians should be committed to memory, written in the mind and heart" (*Sermons and Talks* [Silver Spring, Md.: Ellen G. White Estate, 1994], vol. 2, pp. 119, 120).

11. Promises

"Put away the foolish reading matter and study the Word of God. **Commit its precious promises to memory** so that when we shall be deprived of our Bibles we may still be in possession of the Word of God" (*Manuscript Releases* [Silver Spring, Md.: Ellen G. White Estate, 1990], vol. 10, p. 298, emphasis added).